Wonders

1

Practice Book

McGraw Hill

Alphabet Card Credits: 008 Stockdisc/PunchStock; **024** Photodisc/Getty Images; **040** © Squared Studios/Photodisc/Getty Images; **056** Photographers Choice RF/SuperStock; **072** 97/E+/Getty Images; **088** Pixtal/AGE Fotostock; **104** Stockbyte/Punchstock/Getty Images; **120** Ingram Publishing; **136** Comstock Images/Alamy Stock Photo; **152** Photodisc/Getty Images; **168** Arco Images/Petra Wegner/imageBROKER/Alamy Stock Photo; **184** Westend61/Getty Images; **200** D. Hurst/Alamy Stock Photo; **216** Photodisc/Getty Images; **232** Radlund & Associates/Artville/Getty Images; **248** Siede Preis/Photodisc/Getty Images; **266** Jules Frazier/Photodisc Green/Getty Images; **284** Photo Spin/Alamy Stock Photo; **302** Matthew Cant/ImageState/Alamy Stock Photo; **320** McGraw-Hill Education; **338** Michele Burgess/Corbis; **356** Al Franklin/Corbis; **374** Steve Cole/Photodisc/Getty Images; **392** © Squared Studios/Photodisc/Getty Images; **410** Rubberball Productions/Getty Images; **428** Joshua Ets-Hokin/Photodisc/Getty Images.

mheducation.com/prek-12

McGraw Hill

Send all inquiries to:
McGraw Hill
1325 Avenue of the Americas
New York, NY 10019

ISBN: 978-1-26-579743-0
MHID: 1-26-579743-9

Printed in the United States of America.

7 8 9 10 11 12 SMN 28 27 26 25 24 23 C

Contents

Week 1

Week 2

Week 3

Contents

UNIT 1

Week 1

Week 2

Week 3

Week 4

Week 5

Week 1

Week 2

Week 3

Week 4

Week 5

Week 1

Week 2

Week 3

Week 4

Week 5

Week 1

Week 2

Week 3

Week 4

Week 5

Week 1

Week 2

Week 3

Week 4

Week 5

Week 1

Week 2

Week 3

Week 4

Week 5

Name ______________________________

Listen to the beginning sound in the word **van**. Then listen for the ending part.

Listen to the beginning sound in the word **six**. Then listen for the ending part.

6

Listen to the word parts. Then say the word as a whole. Circle the picture that matches the word you made.

1.

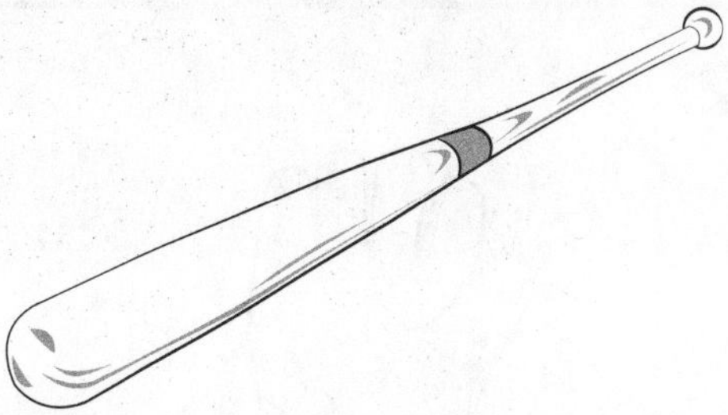

2.

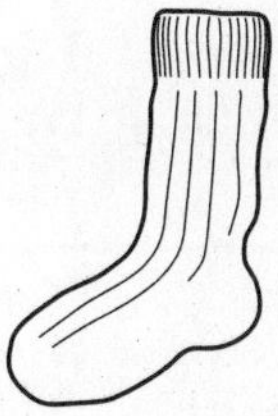

3.

Teacher Directions: Read the box at the top of the page aloud to children. Point to the pictures as you say the words *van* and *six*. Explain that the beginning sound in *van* is /v/, and the ending part is /an/. Then say: *The beginning sound in six is /s/* and *the ending part is /iks/.* Have children listen to the word parts and then say the word as a whole. 1. Say: /p/ /an/. What's the word?; 2. Say: /s/ /ok/. What's the word?; 3. Say: /f/ /ish/. What's the word?

Name ____

Say each picture name out loud. Circle the two pictures of words that have the same beginning sound.

1.

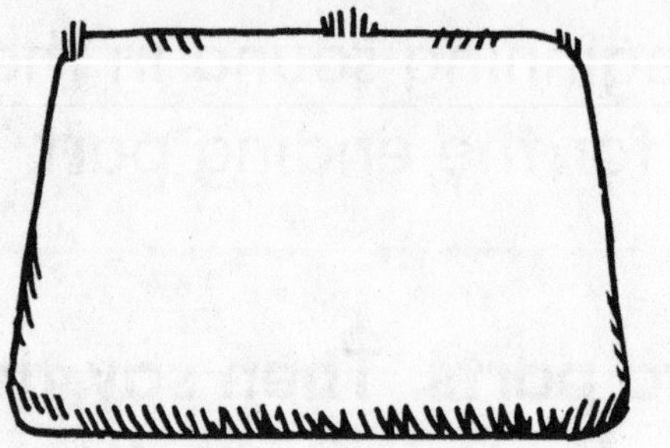

6

2.

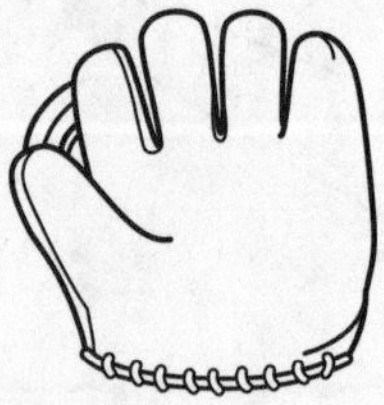

3.

Teacher Directions: Model item 1 by saying /s/ /a/ /d/. *I will blend the sounds to make a word: /sssaaad/, sad.* Then say *mat* and *six*. Stress the /s/ and /m/ beginning sounds. Say: *The words sad and six have the same beginning sound: /s/. Mat has a different beginning sound: /m/.* Guide children to circle the pictures for *sad* and *six*. For items 2–3, say the following sounds. Have students blend the sounds to say each word. Then have them circle the two pictures of words that have the same beginning sound. 2. /m/ /i/ /t/, /m/ /e/ /n/, /s/ /i/ /t/; 3. /m/ /ü/ /n/, /s/ /ü/ /p/, /s/ /u/ /n/.

Name ______________________________

A. Say each picture name. Write m below the picture if its name begins like map. Write s if its name begins like sun.

B. Write m below the picture if its name ends like jam.

Name ____________________

A. Say each picture name. Write a below the picture if its name begins with a as in apple.

B. Say each picture name. Write a to complete the words.

h ____ t

f ____ n

Do you?

Teacher Directions: Review the high-frequency words: *do, I, like, to, you.* Have children read the story. Then have them retell the story using the action words: *swim, read, paint.*

I Like To

I like to  .

I like to .

2

I like to .

3

Name ____

Left-Handed Writers

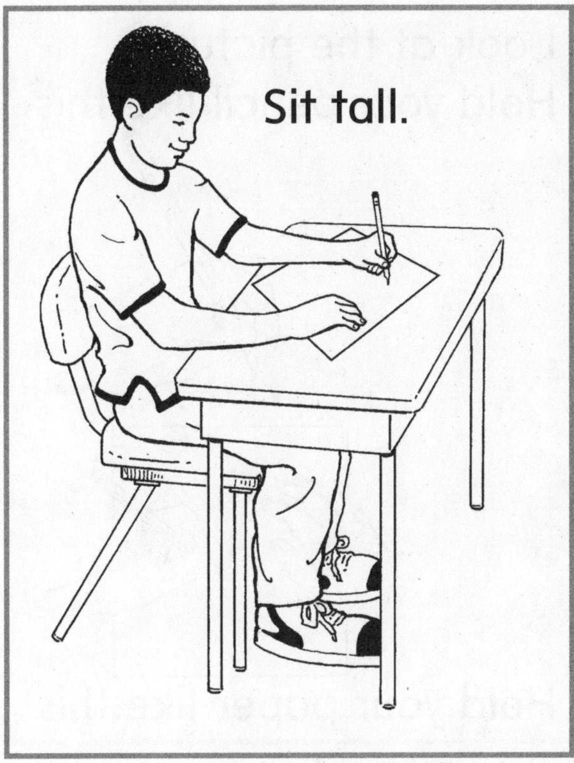

Right-Handed Writers

Look at the pictures. Write your name on the lines below. Make sure you sit correctly as you write. Write neatly.

Name ______________________________

Left-Handed Writers

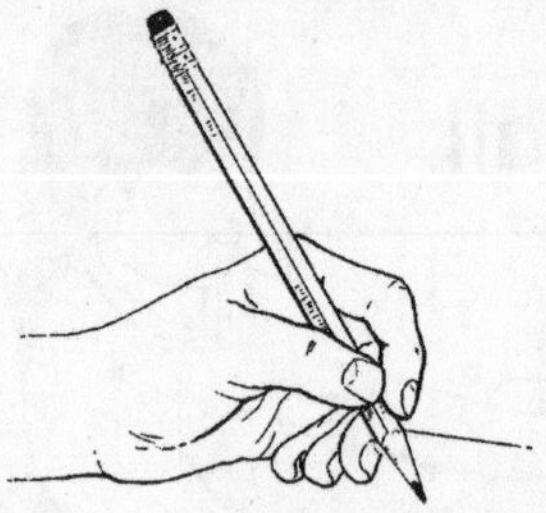

Look at the picture.
Hold your pencil like this.

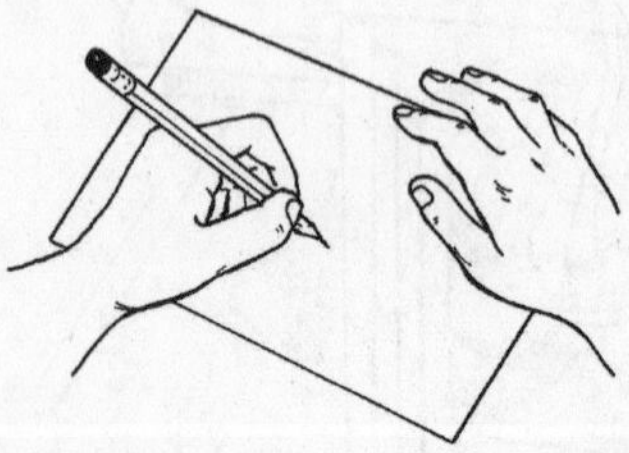

Slant your paper like this.

Right-Handed Writers

Look at the picture.
Hold your pencil like this.

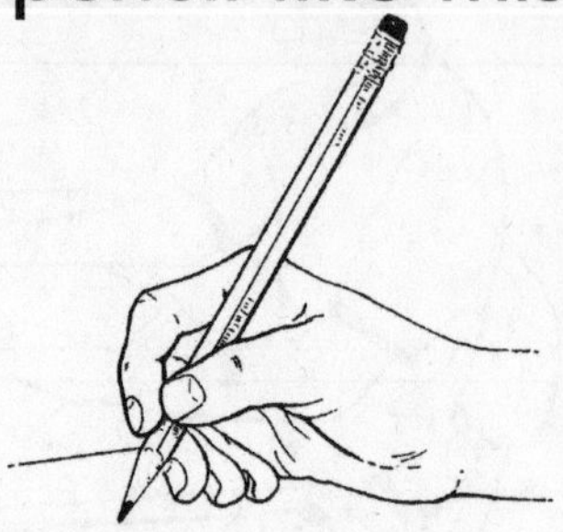

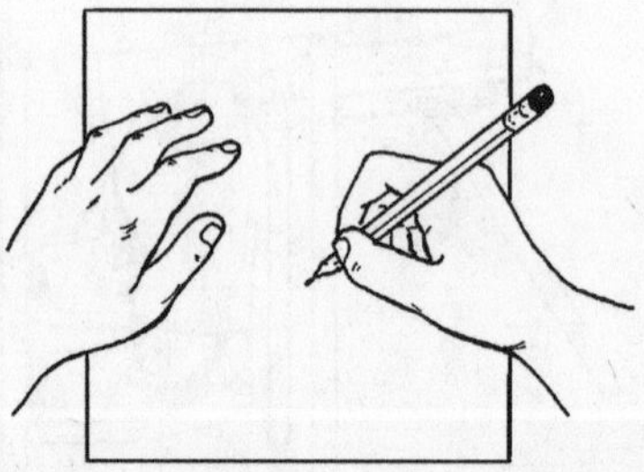

Hold your paper like this.

Look at the pictures. Then write your name. Make sure you hold your pencil and paper correctly. Write neatly.

Name ____________________

Trace and write the letters. Write neatly.

Mm

Mm Mm

Mm

Ss

Ss Ss Ss

Ss

Aa

Aa Aa

Aa

Write a sentence. Leave spaces between the words.

Name ______________________________

A. Say each picture name. Write p below the picture if its name begins like pin. Write t below the picture if its name begins like toy.

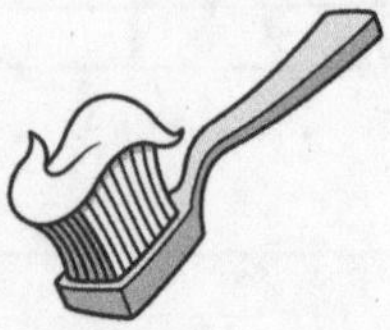

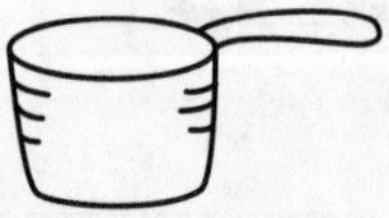

B. Say each picture name. Write p below the picture if its name ends like cup. Write t below the picture if its name ends like bat.

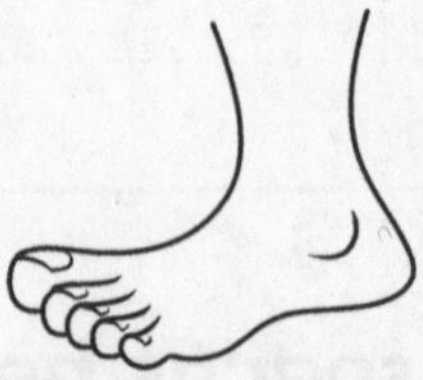

Name ______________________________

A. Say each picture name. Write n below the picture if its name begins like nest. Write r if its name begins like rat.

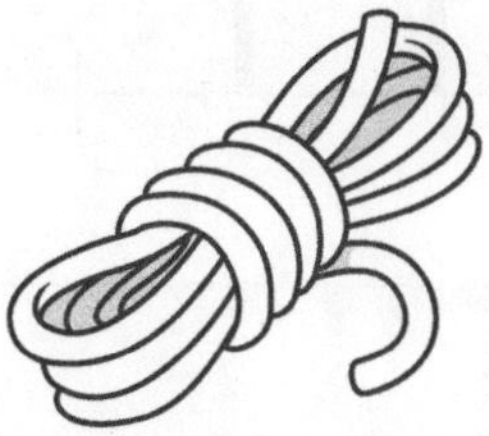

B. Say each picture name. Then write n below the picture if its name ends like fun.

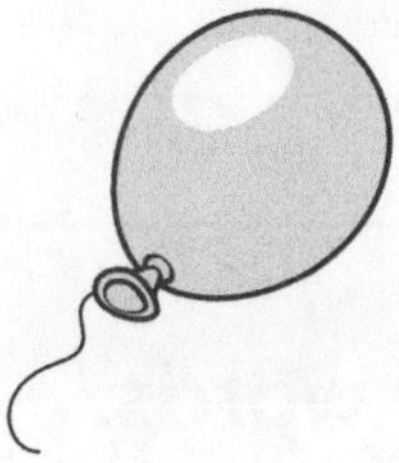

Name ____________________

Trace and write the letters. Write neatly.

Pp

Pp Pp Pp

Pp

Tt

Tt Tt Tt

Tt

Nn

Nn Nn Nn

Nn

Write a sentence. Leave spaces between the words.

He Can Go!

He has a  .

He can go!

Teacher Directions: Review the high-frequency words: *a, can, go, has, he.* Have children read the story. Then have them retell the story using the clothing words: *jacket (or coat), boots, mittens.*

He has 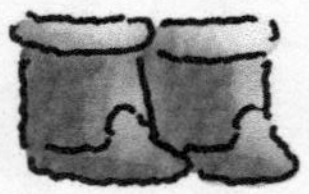 .

2

He has  .

3

Name ______________________________

A. Say each picture name. Write <u>i</u> below the picture if its name begins with <u>i</u> as in <u>ink</u>.

B. Say each picture name. Write <u>i</u> to complete the words.

s ____ x

p ____ g

Name ______________________________

Trace and write the letters. Write neatly.

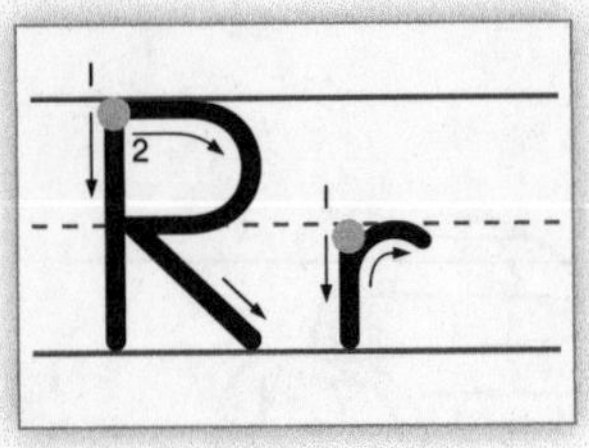

Rr Rr Rr

Rr

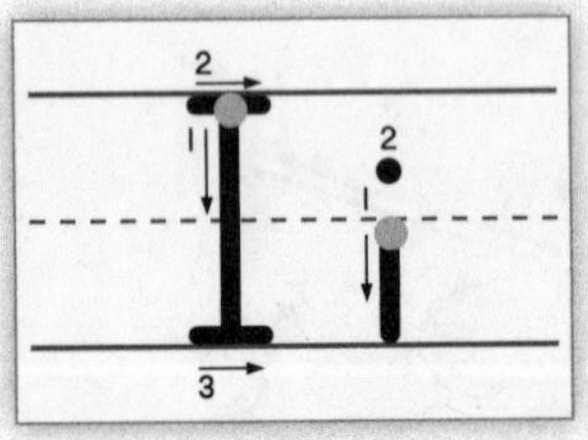

Ii Ii Ii

Ii

Write some sentences. Leave spaces between the words.

Name ______________________________

Say the name of each picture. Count the syllables in each word. Then draw an X in one box for each syllable.

1. 			
2. 			
3. 			
4. 			

Teacher Directions: Model item 1 by saying book. Say: *I can clap the syllables, or word parts, I hear. The word* book *has one syllable:* book. *Clap the syllables with me:* book. *You clapped one time because* book *has one syllable.*

Name ____

Say each picture name. Say the middle sounds. Circle the picture whose name has the same middle sound as the first picture in the row.

1.

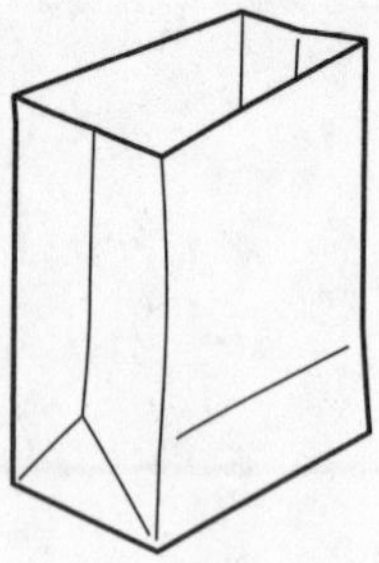

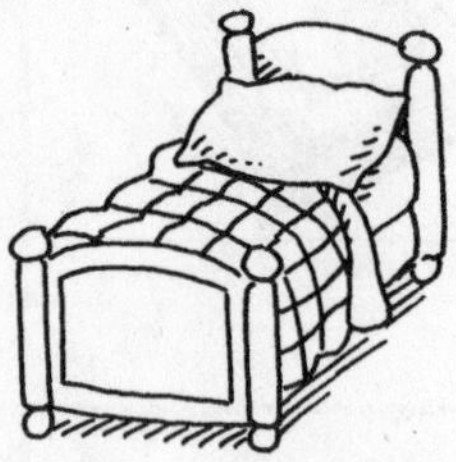

2.

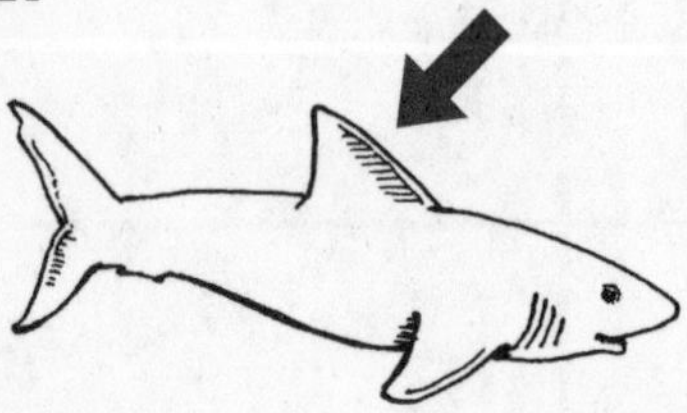

3.

Teacher Directions: Model item 1 by saying /b/ /a/ /g/. Emphasize the middle sound. Then say *map* and *bed* and explicitly compare middle sounds. Say: *The words* bag *and* map *have the same middle sound: /a/.* Bed *has a different middle sound: /e/.* Guide children to circle the picture of the map.

Name ______________________________

A. Say each picture name. Write c below the picture if its name begins like cat. Write f if its name begins like fun.

 ________

 ________

 ________

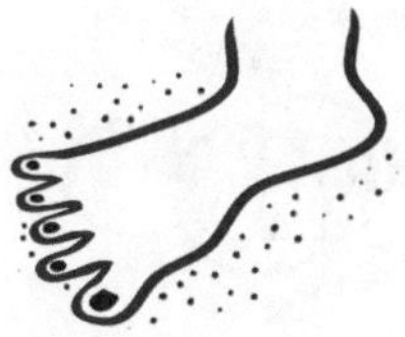 ________

 ________

 ________

B. Write c or f to complete the words.

________ at 

________ an 

Name ______________________

A. Say each picture name. Write o below the picture if its name begins with o as in ox.

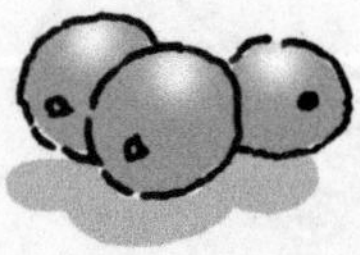

B. Say each picture name. Write o to complete the words.

___ x

b ___ x

This is my !

Teacher Directions: Review the high-frequency words: *is, look, little, my, this.* Have children read the story. Then have them retell the story using the animal words: *giraffe, monkey, bear.*

4

Look!

Look! This is my .

1

Look! This is my  .

2

Look! This is my little  .

3

Name ______________________________

Trace and write the letters. Write neatly.

Cc

Cc Cc Cc

Cc

Ff

Ff Ff Ff

Ff

Oo

Oo Oo

Oo

Write a sentence. Leave spaces between the words.

Name ______________________________

A. Say each picture name. Write d below the picture if its name begins like door. Write h if its name begins like home.

B. Say the picture name. Then write d to complete the word. Read the word.

b e ______

Name ______________________________

A. Say each picture name. Write e below the picture if its name begins with e as in egg.

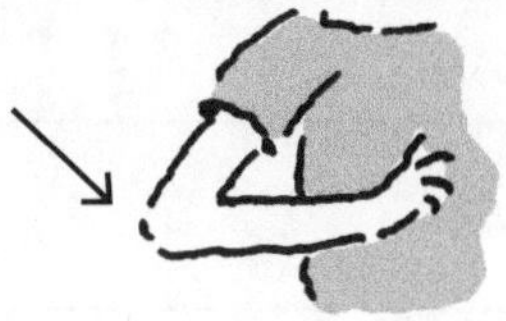

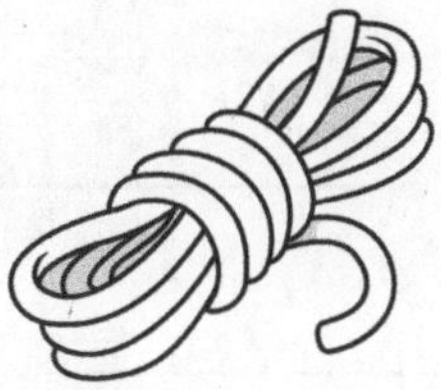

B. Say the picture name. Then write e to complete the word. Read the word.

l ____ g

Name ______________________________

Trace and write the letters. Write neatly.

Dd  Dd Dd Dd

Dd

Hh  Hh Hh Hh

Hh

Ee  Ee Ee Ee

Ee

Write a sentence. Leave spaces between the words.

This is where we play!

Teacher Directions: Review the high-frequency words: *and, have, said, see, was.* Have children read the story. Then have them retell the story using the position words: *off, down, up.*

We Play Here

The  play here.

The  play here.

The  play here.

Name ______________________________

A. Say each picture name. Write <u>b</u> below the picture if its name begins like <u>bat</u>. Write <u>l</u> if its name begins like <u>lemon</u>.

B. Say the picture name. Then write <u>b</u> to complete the word. Read the word.

t u ______

Name ______________________________

Trace and write the letters. Write neatly.

Bb

Bb Bb Bb

Bb

Ll

Ll Ll Ll Ll

Ll

Write some sentences. Leave spaces between the words.

Name ____

Listen to the sounds your teacher says. Put the sounds together. Draw a picture of the word you made.

1.	**2.**
3.	**4.**

Teacher Directions: Model item 1 by saying */m/ /a/ /n/. Listen as I blend these three sounds: /mmmaaannn/, man.* Model drawing a man in the first box and have children copy. For items 2–4, have children listen to the sounds and blend them to form a word. 2. Say: /p/ /e/ /n/; 3. Say: /m/ /o/ /p/; 4. Say: /f/ /a/ /n/.

Name ______________________________

Say the name of each picture. Count the sounds in each word. Then draw an X in one box for each sound.

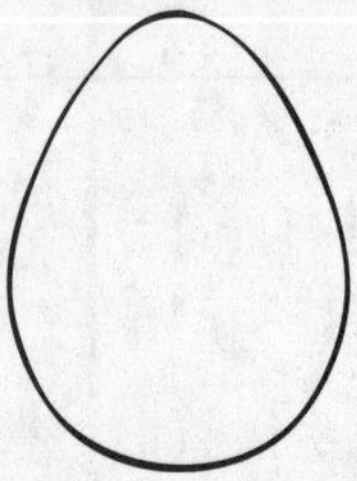

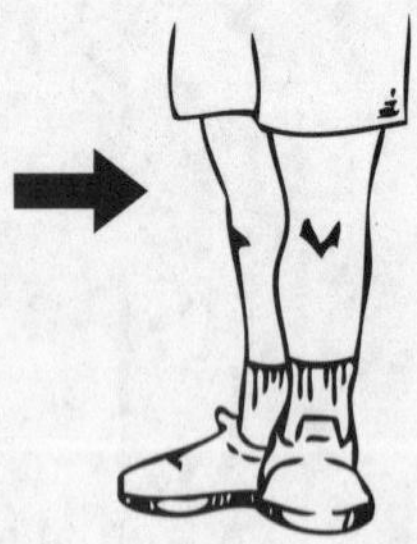

Teacher Directions: Model item 1 by saying egg. Say: *I can say the sounds in the word* egg. *The word* egg *has two sounds: /e/ /g/. Say the sounds with me: /e/ /g/.*

Name ______________________________

A. Say each picture name. Write <u>k</u> below the picture if its name begins like <u>king</u>.

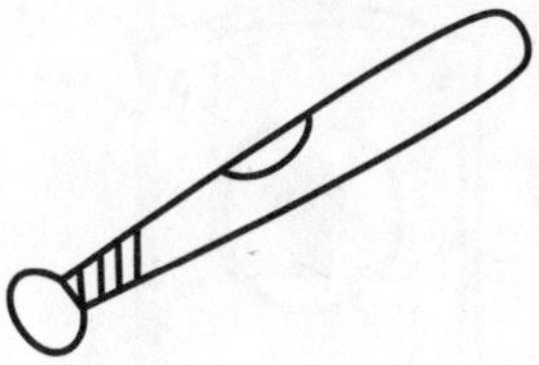

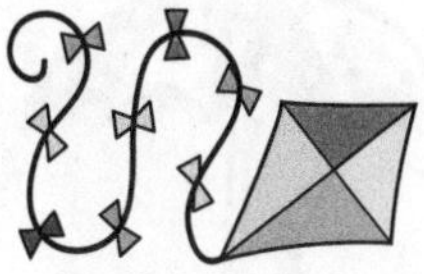

B. Say each picture name. Write <u>ck</u> below the picture if its name ends like <u>back</u>.

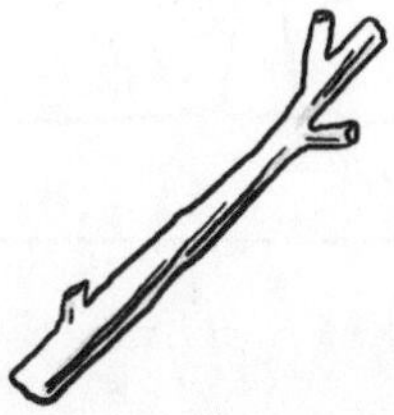

C. Write the letters <u>ck</u> to make new words.

ki ______________ so ______________

Name ______________________________

A. Say each picture name. Write u below the picture if its name begins with u as in up.

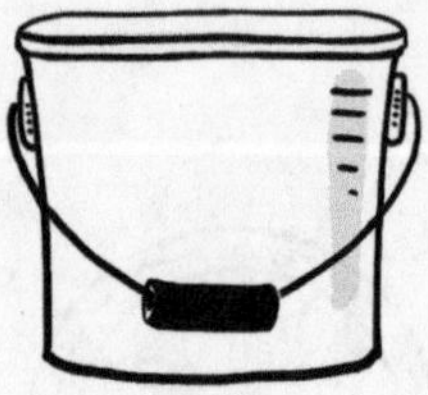

B. Say the picture name. Then write u to complete the word. Read the word.

c ______ p

She has a  for me!

Teacher Directions: Review the high-frequency words: *are, for, me, she, with.* Have children read the story. Then have them retell the story using the position words: *in front of, behind, next to.*

4

With Me

Look! I can go.

1

She is with me.

We are here.

Name ____

Trace and write the letters. Write neatly.

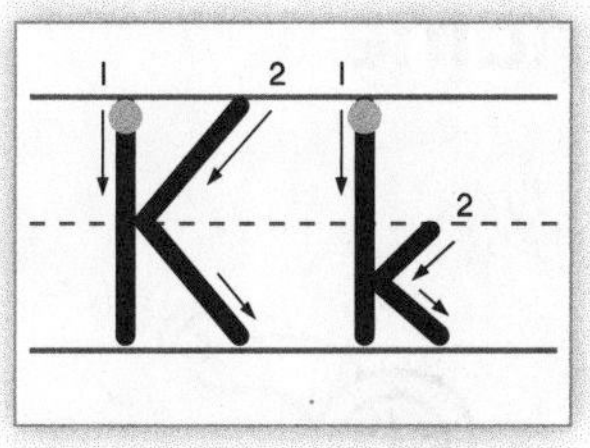

K k K k K k

K k

U u U u U u

U u

G g G g

G g

Write a sentence. Leave spaces between the words.

____

Name ________________________________

A. Say each picture name. Write g below the picture if its name begins like gate. Write w if its name begins like water.

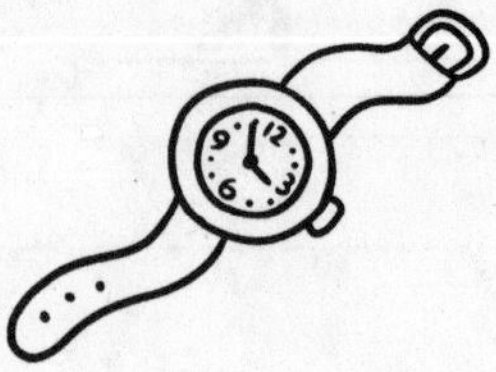

B. Say each picture name. Then write g below the picture if its name ends like dog.

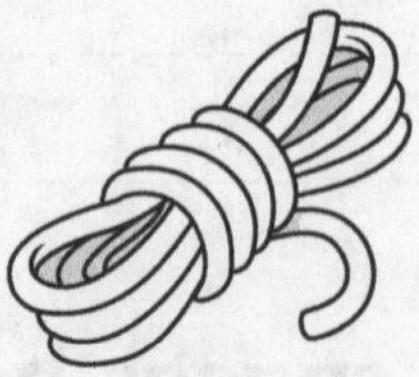

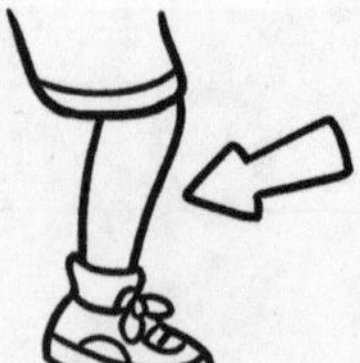

Name ______________________________

A. Say each picture name. Write q below the picture if its name begins like quick. Write v if its name begins like van.

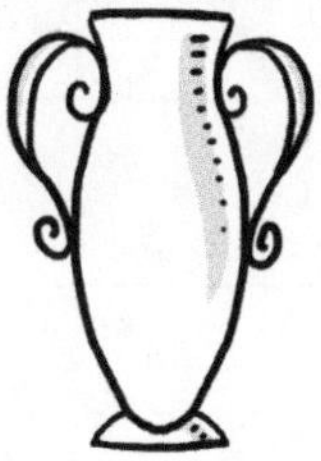

B. Say each picture name. Then write x below the picture if its name ends like fox.

Name ______________________________

Trace and write the letters. Write neatly.

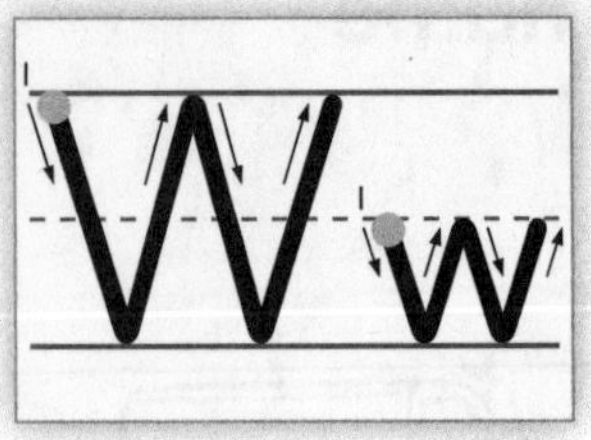

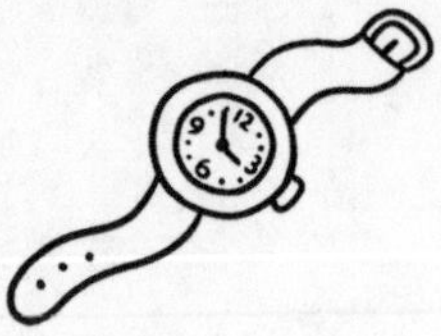

Ww Ww

Ww

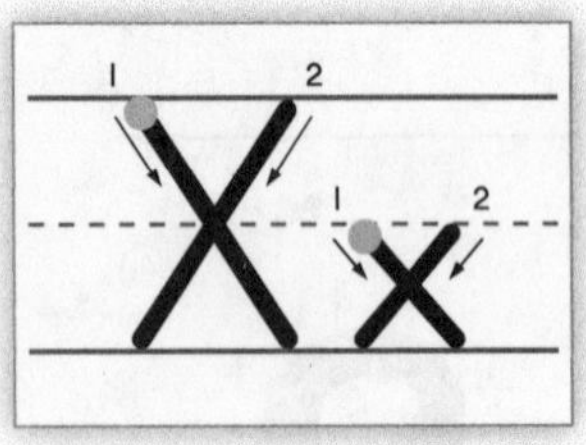

Xx Xx Xx

Xx

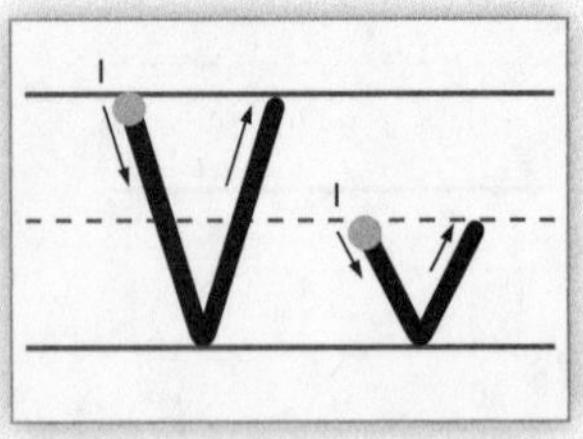

Vv Vv Vv

Vv

Write a sentence. Leave spaces between the words.

He and she go!

Teacher Directions: Review the high-frequency words: *and, have, said, see, was.* Have children read the story. Then have them retell the story using the position words: *off, down, up.*

④

He and She Go

He was .

①

"Have this," she said.

②

See! He is .

③

Name ____________________________________

A. Say each picture name. Write j below the picture if its name begins like jam. Write y if its name begins like yarn. Write z if its name begins like zoo.

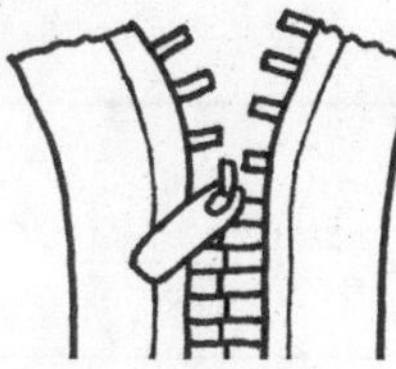

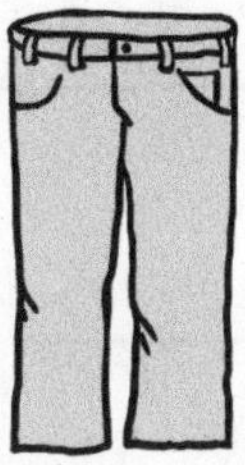

B. Write j, y, or z to complete the words.

0

___ero ___arn ___am

Name ______________________________

Trace and write the letters. Write neatly.

Qq

Qq Qq

Qq

Jj

Jj Jj Jj

Jj

Yy

Yy Yy Yy

Yy

Zz

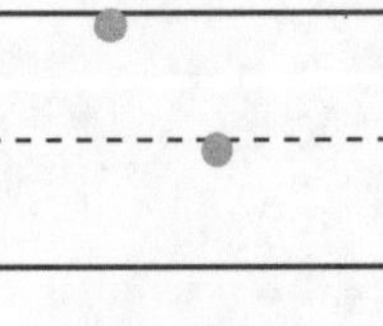

Zz Zz Zz

Zz

Name ______________________________

Words that rhyme end with the same sounds.

Say the name of each picture. Circle the two pictures that rhyme in each row.

1.

2.

3.

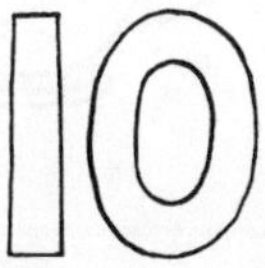

4.

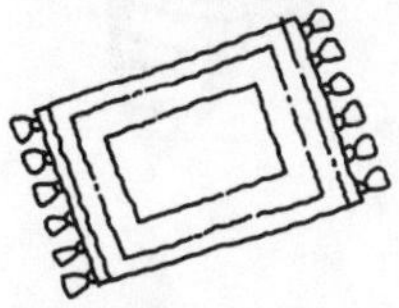

5.

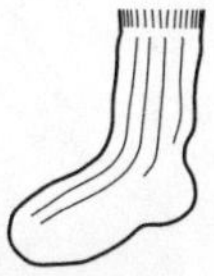

Teacher Directions: Read the box at the top of the page aloud. Point to the pictures as you name each one: *fan, pan.* Emphasize the ending sounds. Explain that these two words rhyme.

Name ______________________________

Say each picture name. Say the beginning sound. Circle the picture whose name has the same beginning sound as the first picture in the row.

1.			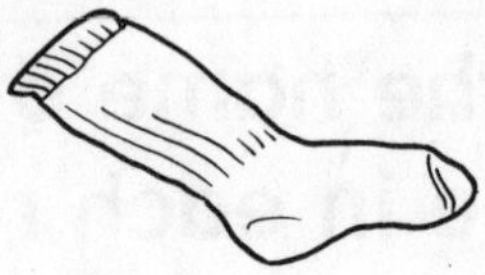
2.		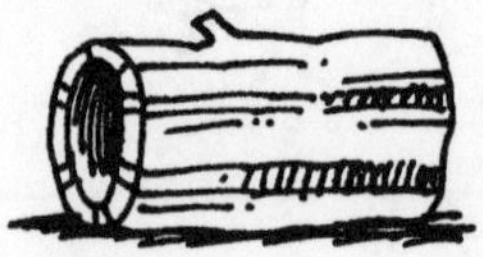	
3.			
4.		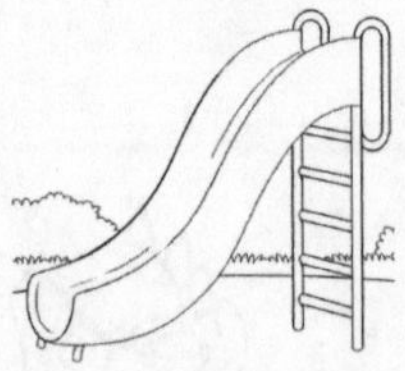	
5.			

Teacher Directions: Model item 1 by pointing to the *duck* and telling children that the word *duck* begins with the /d/ sound. Then explain that the word *dog* begins with /d/ and *sock* begins with /s/. Say: *The words* duck *and* dog *have the same beginning sound: /d/.* Sock *has a different beginning sound: /s/.* Guide children to circle the picture of the dog.

Name ____

The letter <u>**a**</u> stands for the short **a** sound you hear in **h<u>a</u>t**.

Read the word. Listen for the short <u>a</u> sound. Circle the picture that the word names.

1. fan		
2. cat		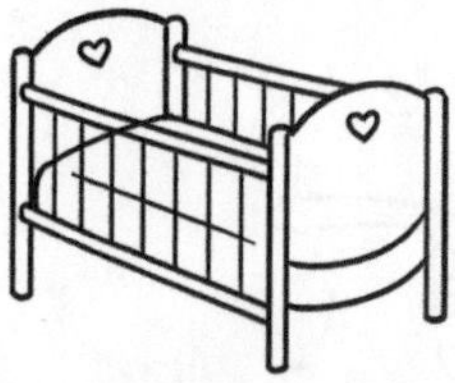
3. pan		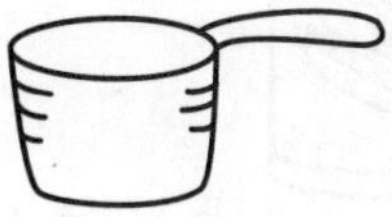
4. map	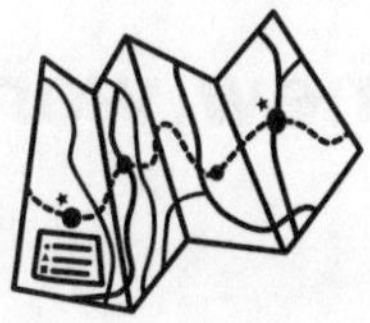	

Name ____________________

A. Read the words in the box. Write the word that names the picture.

bat	can	hat	pan

1.  ____________________

2. 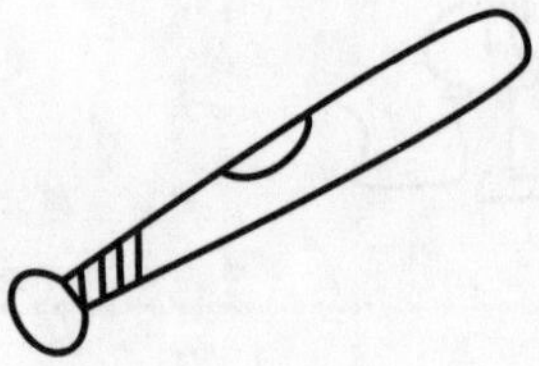 ____________________

3. 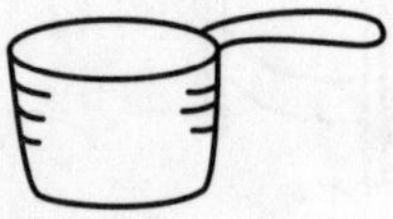 ____________________

4.  ____________________

B. Change one letter to make a new word with the short a sound. Then write the word.

1. men ____________________ **2.** fin ____________________

Name ____________________

Fold back the paper along the dotted line. Use the blanks to write each word as it is read aloud. When you finish the test, unfold the paper. Use the list at the right to correct any spelling mistakes.

1. ____________________ **1. man**

2. ____________________ **2. can**

3. ____________________ **3. nap**

4. ____________________ **4. tap**

5. ____________________ **5. cat**

6. ____________________ **6. hat**

High-Frequency Words

7. ____________________ **7. not**

8. ____________________ **8. does**

Name ______________________________

A. Read the words in the box. Then sort the words using the word endings.

can	nap	man	hat	tap	cat

Words with ap	**Words with an**	**Words with at**

B. Think of words that have the same word endings. Add them to the chart.

Name ______________________________

A. Read the words in the box. Then sort the words using the word endings.

can	cat	man	mat

Words with an	**Words with at**

B. Think of words that have the same word endings. Add them to the chart.

Name ______________________________

A. Read the words in the box. Then sort the words.

can cat flat hat man nap tap that

Words with <u>an</u>	**Words with <u>at</u>**	**Words with <u>ap</u>**

B. Think of new words to add to the chart.

Name ______________________________

man	can	nap	tap
cat	hat	not	does

Look at the picture. Use a spelling word to complete the sentence.

1. Do you see the ______________________ ?

2. She does ______________________ nap.

3. The ______________________ has a bag.

4. I like this ______________________ .

5. He can ______________________ .

Name ____________________

Trace and write A and a. Then copy the sentence. Make sure to leave spaces between words.

Aa

A A A A A A

A A A

a a a a a a a a a

a a a

Amy ate an apple.

Name ______________________________

Add -<u>s</u> to an action word when it follows a name or the words **he**, **she**, or **it**. Read the words. Listen for the sounds at the end of **naps**.

I nap. **He nap<u>s</u>.** **Pam nap<u>s</u>.**

Circle the word that completes each sentence. Then write the word. Read the sentences.

1. It ____________________.

quack quacks

2. Max ____________________ for school.

pack packs

3. He ____________________.

bat bats

Name ______________________________

A. Circle the word that completes each sentence.

1. She (pat, pats) Max.

2. Pam (bag, bags) it.

3. It (yap, yaps).

4. The cat (nap, naps).

B. Use one of the words you circled above to write a new sentence.

____

____

Name ______________________________

A. Read and spell each word in the box. Complete each sentence. Use one of the words in the box.

does	not	school	what

1. I like my ______________ .

2. Where ______________ Nan go?

3. Sam can ______________ see the map.

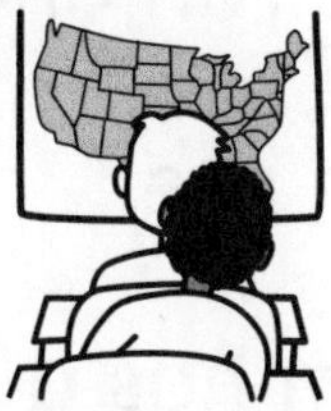

4. ______________ do the cats have?

B. Write your own sentence using a word from the box.

____

____

Teacher Directions: Point to the word *does.* Use the Read/Spell/Write routine. Repeat for each word in the box.

Name ______________________________

A **sentence** is a group of words that tells a whole idea.
A sentence begins with a capital letter.

Example: Nat can go.

A. Circle the sentences.

1. Sam has a hat.
2. like to.
3. We ran and ran.
4. can see.
5. Pam has a bag.
6. Nan can play.
7. A cat.

**B. Add words to make this a sentence.
Write the sentence.**

1. _____ can hop.

____

Name ______________________________

A. Read the draft model. Find the errors.

Draft Model

A cat.

Sam likes to.

B. Revise the draft by fixing the errors you found. Make sure each sentence tells a whole idea.

____

____

____

____

____

Connect to Writing

C. Look in your writer's notebook. Make sure you used complete sentences.

Name ______________________________

Every sentence begins with a capital letter.

Write each sentence correctly.

1. sam is at school. ______________________

2. you can go with me. ______________________

3. a cat can not go. ______________________

4. this is my cat. ______________________

5. dan can go too. ______________________

Jack likes to nap.

Connect to Community: Have children talk to a family member about pets they know.

(4)

Jack the Cat

Jack is a cat.

Teacher Directions: Have children establish a purpose for reading the take-home story.

(1)

Jack likes to play.

2

Jack likes Tam.

3

Name ______________________________

Alliteration is when you repeat the beginning sound in two or more words.

Example: Lily likes lemons.

Listen to the sentences your teacher says. Circle the picture of the sentence with alliteration.

1.

2.

3.

Teacher Directions: Read the box at the top of the page aloud. Read the sample sentence and emphasize the /l/ sounds at the beginning of each word. Explain that this sentence is an example of alliteration. Point to each picture as you read each sentence. 1. Say: *Pam pats.* Then say: *Nick ran.* 2. Say: *Tam hits.* Then say: *Tim taps.* 3. Say: *Sam sits.* Then say: *It quacks.*

Name ____

Listen to the sounds your teacher says. Blend the sounds together. Draw a picture of the word you made.

1.	**2.**
3.	**4.**

Teacher Directions: Model item 1 by saying */p/ /i/ /g/. Listen as I blend these sounds together: /piiig/, pig.* Model drawing a pig in the first box and have children copy. For items 2–4, have children listen to the sounds and blend them to form a word. 2. Say: /m/ /i/ /t/; 3. Say: /w/ /i/ /g/; 4. Say: /s/ /t/ /i/ /k/.

Name ____

The letter i stands for the short **i** sound
you hear in **pin**.

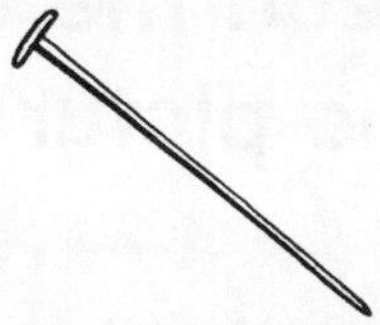

Read the word. Listen for the short i sound. Circle the picture that the word names.

1. hill

2. pig

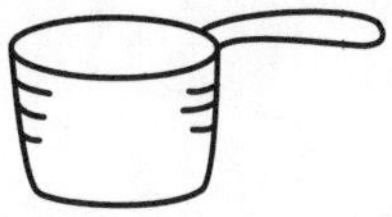

3. fin

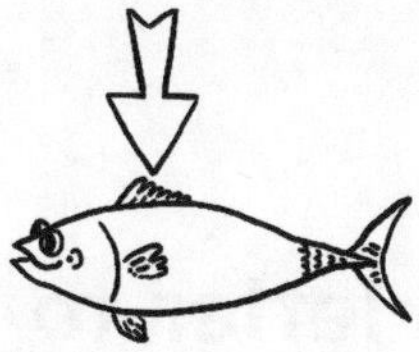

4. lid

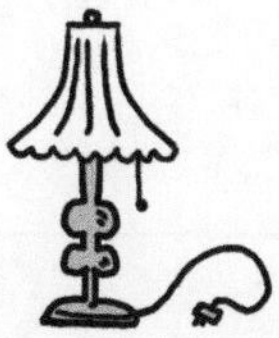

Name ______________________

A. Read the words in the box. Write the word that names the picture.

kiss	pin	pick	dig	win

1.  ______________

2. 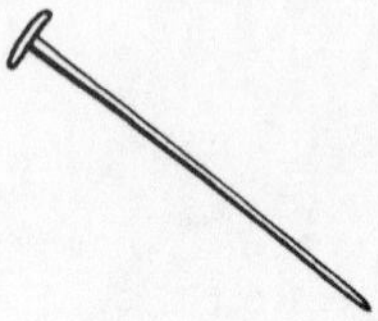 ______________

3.  ______________

B. Change one letter to make a new word with the short <u>i</u> sound. Then write the word.

1. bag ______________ 2. hat ______________

3. fan ______________ 4. pack ______________

Name ______________________________

Fold back the paper along the dotted line. Use the blanks to write each word as it is read aloud. When you finish the test, unfold the paper. Use the list at the right to correct any spelling mistakes.

1. ______________ **1. pin**

2. ______________ **2. win**

3. ______________ **3. hit**

4. ______________ **4. sit**

5. ______________ **5. miss**

6. ______________ **6. kiss**

High-Frequency Words

7. ______________ **7. out**

8. ______________ **8. up**

Name ______________________________

A. Read the words in the box. Then sort the words using the word endings.

hit	kiss	miss	pin	sit	win

Words with <u>iss</u>	Words with <u>it</u>	Words with <u>in</u>

B. Think of words that have the same word endings. Add them to the chart.

Name ______________________________

A. Read the words in the box. Then sort the words using the word endings.

hit	pin	sit	win

Words with <u>in</u>	**Words with <u>it</u>**
____________	____________
____________	____________
____________	____________
____________	____________

B. Think of words that have the same word endings. Add them to the chart.

Name ______________________________

A. Read the words in the box. Then sort the words.

hit	kiss	skin	pin
sit	spin	miss	win

Words with <u>iss</u>	Words with <u>it</u>	Words with <u>in</u>

B. Think of words that have the same word endings. Add them to the chart.

Name ______________________________

pin	win	hit	sit	miss
kiss	nap	can	out	up

A. Write the spelling word that names the picture.

1. ______________________

2. ______________________

B. Write the word that completes the sentence.

3. He ______________________ it!

4. I go ______________________ .

5. Can she ______________________ ?

Name ______________________________

Trace and write <u>I</u> and <u>i</u>. Then copy the sentence. Make sure to leave spaces between words.

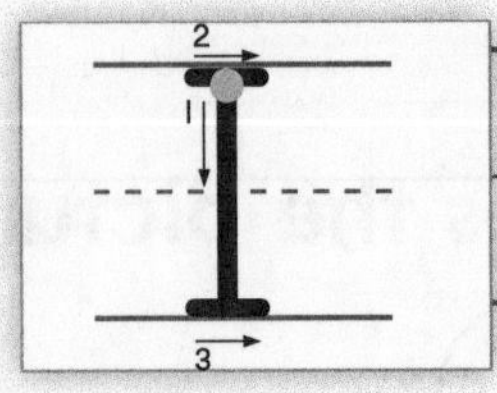

I I I I I

I

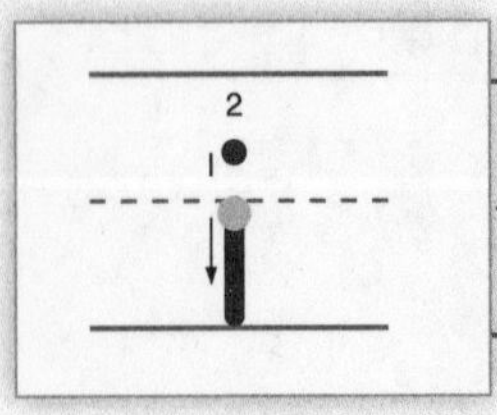

i i i i i i i i

i

Ida is in the igloo.

Name ______________________________

When a word ends with two consonants that are the same, the letters together make one sound.

will **jazz** **pass**

Read each sentence. Underline the word that ends with the same two consonants. Write the word on the line.

1. Cam will hit. ______________________

2. Dan can pass. ______________________

3. Matt has a big hat. ______________________

4. Pam has to miss school. ______________________

Name ______________________________

A. Circle the word that completes each sentence.

1. She can (fill, fil) it.

2. Mom can (kis, kiss) Sam.

3. We (will, wil) play.

B. Use one of the words you circled above to write a new sentence.

____

____

Name ____________________

A. Read and spell each word in the box. Complete each sentence. Use one of the words in the box.

down	out	up	very

1. I go ____________________ to play.

2. Sam sits ____________________ .

3. The bag is ____________________ big.

4. Look ____________________ at my cat.

B. Use a word from the box to write your own sentence.

____

Teacher Directions: Point to the word *down*. Use the Read/Spell/Write routine. Repeat for each word in the box.

Name ______________________________

The words in a sentence must be in the right order.

The order must make sense.

Correct: Tim has a tan cap.

Not correct: cap a has Tim tan.

A. Circle the sentences that have the words in the right order.

1. tag can Dan play.

2. Bill can go here.

3. cat hid The bag in a.

4. Sam is a big pig.

5. Sid and Pat can go.

B. Write your own sentence. Check that your words are in the right order from left to right.

____

Name ______________________________

A. Read the draft model. Find the errors.

Draft Model

at Sam Look.

is my He pal.

B. Revise the draft by fixing the errors you found. Make sure the words are in the right order.

Connect to Writing

C. Look in your writer's notebook. Make sure your sentences are in correct word order.

Name ______________________________

Every sentence ends with a punctuation mark.

Example: Sal can sit here.

Put a period at the end of each sentence.
Circle the mark.

1. I see a tan bag ______________

2. A cat can play ______________

3. Tab hid in the bag ______________

4. She is not sad ______________

5. Tab can go in ______________

6. She can go out ______________

Tip will sit.

Connect to Community: Have children talk to a family member about activities they like to do with friends.

4

Pip and Tip

Pip will go up.

Teacher Directions: Have children establish a purpose for reading the take-home story.

1

Tip will not go up.

2

Pip will dig.

3

Name ______________________________

Listen to the sounds your teacher says. Blend them together to make a word. Circle the picture that matches the word you made.

1.

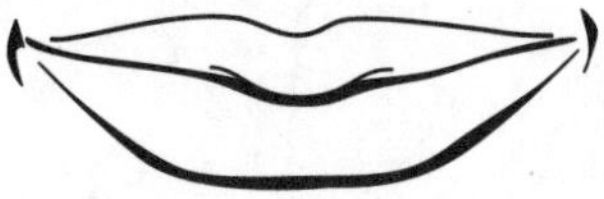

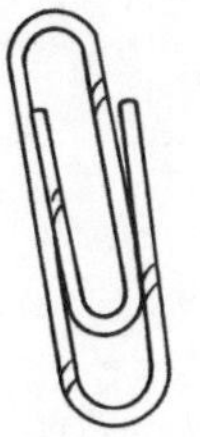

2.

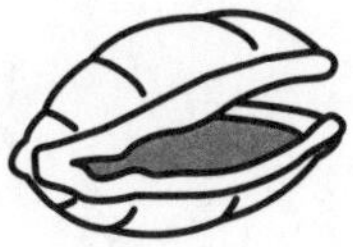

3.

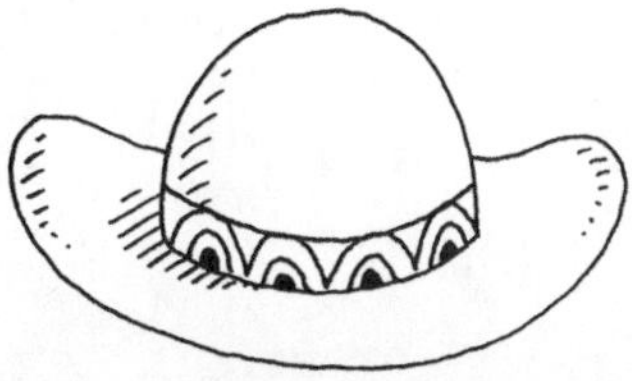

4.

5.

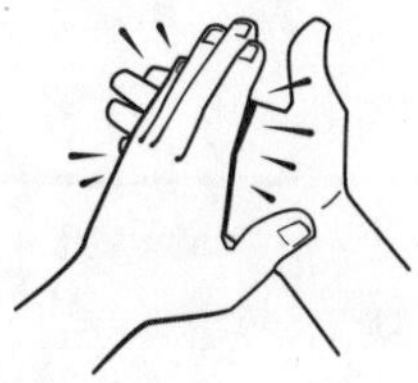

Teacher Directions: 1. Model: *When we say the word* clip, *we blend the sounds of the letters* c *and* l *together: /kl/. Listen as I blend the sounds to say the word: /k/ /l/ /i/ /p/, klip.* 2. Say: /k/ /l/ /a/ /m/, clam; 3. Say: /k/ /a/ /t/, cat; 4. Say: /f/ /l/ /a/ /g/, flag; 5. Say: /k/ /l/ /a/ /p/, clap.

Name ______________________________

Listen to the sounds your teacher says. Blend the sounds together. Draw a picture of the word you made.

1.	**2.**
3.	**4.**

Teacher Directions: Model item 1 saying */k/ /l/ /i/ /p/. Listen as I blend these sounds together: /klllliiip/, clip.* Model drawing a clip in the first box and have children copy. For items 2–4, have children listen to the sounds and blend them to form a word. 2. Say: /f/ /l/ /a/ /g/; 3. Say: /v/ /a/ /n/; 4. Say: /k/ /l/ /a/ /p/.

Name ______________________________

Sometimes consonants form a **blend**. You can hear the sound of a consonant and letter l form a blend at the beginning of **glad** and **slim**.

Read the word. Draw a line under the letters that form a blend. Write the letters. Circle the picture.

1. flag ____________________

2. clip ____________________

3. slip ____________________

4. clam ____________________

Name ____________________

A. Read each word in the box. Use a word from the box to complete each sentence.

clap	flag	slam	black	glad

1. We are ____________________.

2. Matt and Kim ____________________.

3. Do not ____________________ the door!

4. I can see a ____________________.

B. Add one letter to make a new word with a blend. Then write the word.

1. back ____________________ 2. sip ____________________

Name ______________________________

Fold back the paper along the dotted line. Use the blanks to write each word as it is read aloud. When you finish the test, unfold the paper. Use the list at the right to correct any spelling mistakes.

1. ______________ 1. clip
2. ______________ 2. flip
3. ______________ 3. slip
4. ______________ 4. flag
5. ______________ 5. black
6. ______________ 6. plan

High-Frequency Words

7. ______________ 7. be
8. ______________ 8. pull

Name ____________________

A. Read the words in the box. Then sort the words.

black	clip	flag	flip	plan	slip

Words with <u>cl</u>	Words with <u>bl</u>	Words with <u>pl</u>
____________	____________	____________
____________	____________	____________
____________	____________	____________

Words with <u>fl</u>	Words with <u>sl</u>	
____________	____________	
____________	____________	
____________	____________	

B. Think of words that have the same word blends. Add them to the chart.

Name ______________________________

A. Read the words in the box. Then sort the words using the word blends.

clap	flip	clip	slip

Words with <u>cl</u>	Words with <u>sl</u>	Words with <u>fl</u>

B. Think of words that have the same word blends. Add them to the chart.

Name ____________________

A. Read the words in the box. Then sort the words.

black clip glass flag place flip plan slip

Words with <u>cl</u>	**Words with <u>bl</u>**	**Words with <u>pl</u>**

Words with <u>fl</u>	**Words with <u>sl</u>**	**Words with <u>gl</u>**

B. Think of new words to add to the chart.

Name ______________________________

Read each word in the box. Say each word.

clip	flip	slip	flag
black	plan	miss	win

Use the clues to write a spelling word on the line.

1. starts like **flick** + ends like **sip** ______________

2. starts like **flat** + ends like **bag** ______________

3. starts like **blot** + ends like **sack** ______________

4. starts like **slim** + ends like **tip** ______________

5. starts like **cliff** + ends like **lip** ______________

Name ______________________________

Trace and write L and l. Then copy the sentence. Make sure to leave spaces between words.

Ll

L L L L L

L

l l l l l l l l

l

Lily likes lemons.

Name ______________________________

Some words end with s. When a word ends in one s, it means there is more than one of something.

flag 

flags 

Read each sentence. Underline the word that tells about more than one thing. Write the word on the line.

1. See the hats? ____________

2. The fish has fins. ____________

3. We have cats. ____________

4. Tim and Jim have six bats. ____________

Name ______________________________

A. Read the sentences out loud. Circle the word that completes each sentence. Use the pictures to help you.

1. There is a (pin, pins).

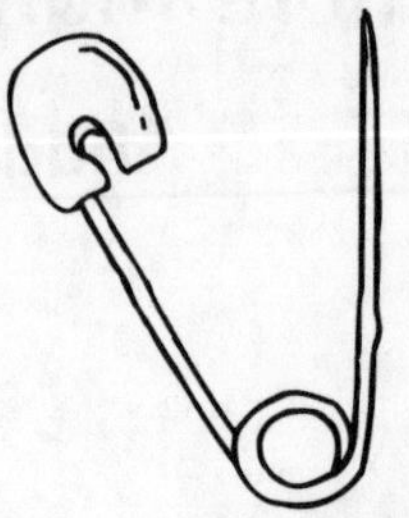

2. Pam has a (bat, bats)

3. He has (hat, hats).

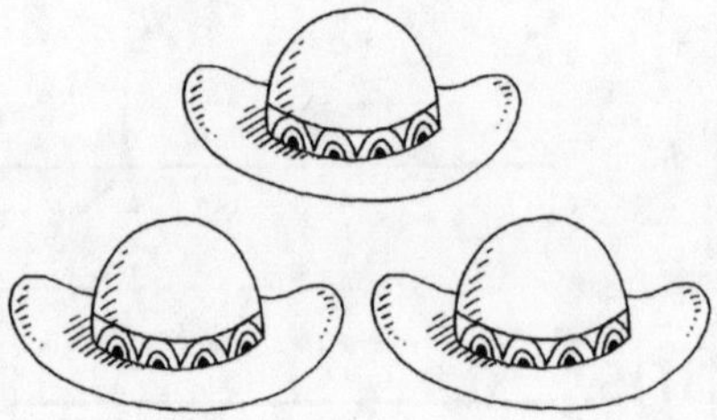

B. Use one of the words you circled to write your own sentence.

____

____

Name ______________________________

A. Read and spell each word in the box. Complete each sentence. Use one of the words in the box.

be	come	good	pull

1. Tam is a ____________ cat.

2. I can ____________ a big help.

3. Max can ____________ the big pig.

4. Tip can ____________ to me.

B. Write your own sentence using a word from the box.

____

Teacher Directions: Point to the word *be*. Use the Read/Spell/Write routine. Repeat for each word in the box.

Name ____

A **statement** tells something.

A statement begins with a capital letter and ends with a period.

Example: Pip can wag.

A **question** is a sentence that asks something. It ends with a question mark.

Example: Can Pip run?

Draw a line under the statements. Circle the questions.

1. Pip and I play.

2. A cat is

3. Can Pip run?

4. He likes to dig.

5. my pal.

6. Can Pip nap?

Name ______________________________

A. Read the draft model. Find the errors.

Draft Model

jack is my pal

can we play

B. Revise the draft by fixing the errors. Remember to include capital letters. Add periods at the end of statements. Add question marks to questions.

Connect to Writing

C. Look in your writer's notebook. Make sure your sentences begin with capital letters and end with periods or question marks.

Name ______________________________

A statement or question begins with a capital letter.

A statement ends with a period. A question ends with a question mark.

Correct each statement or question.

1. Tip is my cat

____

2. can Tip play with me

____

3. can we have fun

____

4. we run up and down

____

Kim is very glad.

Connect to Community: Have children talk to a family member about games they like to play with friends.

Kim and Flick

Flick the cat hid.

Teacher Directions: Have children establish a purpose for reading the take-home story.

Where is Flick?

2

Come out, Flick!

3

Name ____

Say each picture name and the sound that ends it. Circle the picture in each row whose name does NOT end with the same sound as the other two.

1.
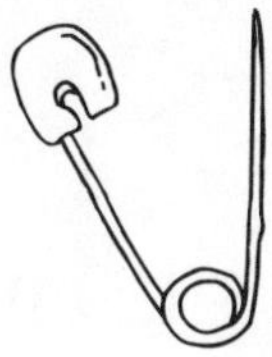
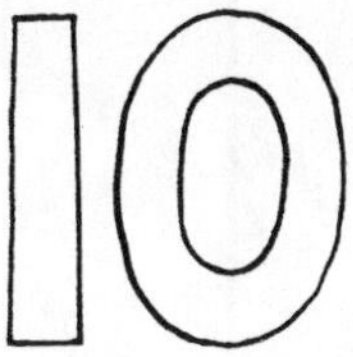

2.

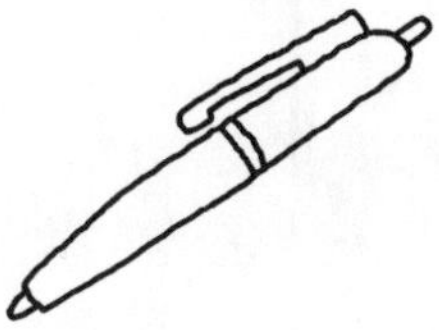

3.

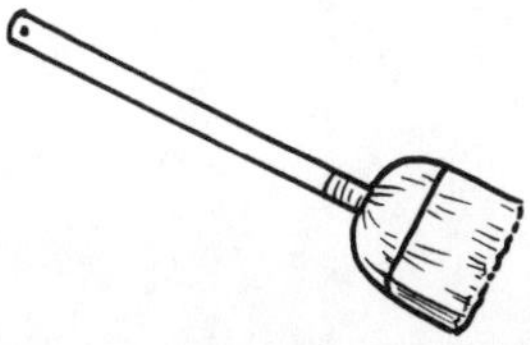

4.

5.

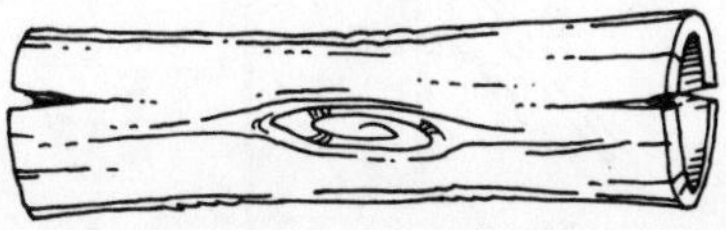

Teacher Directions: Model item 1 by saying *pin, ten,* and *pig.* Repeat, stressing the difference between the /n/ and /g/ ending sounds. Say: *The words* pin *and* ten *have the same ending sound: /n/.* Pig *has a different ending sound: /g/.* Guide children to circle the picture of the pig.

Name ____

Say the name of each picture. Count the sounds in the word. Draw an X in one box for each sound.

1. 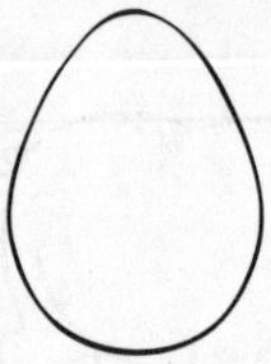			
2. 			
3. 			
4. 			
5. 			

Teacher Directions: Model item 1 by saying *egg.* Say: *I can say the sounds in the word* egg. *The word* egg *has two sounds: /e/ /g/. Say the sounds with me: /e/ /g/.* Guide children to draw two X's for item 1.

Name ______________________________

The letter o stands for the short **o** sound you hear in **sock** and **dot**.

A. Read the words in the box. Listen for the short o sound. Write the word that names each picture.

mop hop clock box

1. ____________ 

2. ____________ 

3. ____________ 

4. ____________ 

B. Circle and write each word that has the short o sound.

5. can mom clip ____________

6. fin mat top ____________

Name ______________________________

A. Read the words in the box. Write the word that names the picture.

ox	block	log	lock	mop	mom

I. 

____

2.  ______________

3.  ______________

4.  ______________

B. Change one letter to make a new word with the short o sound. Then write the word.

I. leg ______________ 2. pit ______________

Name ______________________________

Fold back the paper along the dotted line. Use the blanks to write each word as it is read aloud. When you finish the test, unfold the paper. Use the list at the right to correct any spelling mistakes.

1. ____________ 1. hop
2. ____________ 2. top
3. ____________ 3. log
4. ____________ 4. hog
5. ____________ 5. hot
6. ____________ 6. lot

High-Frequency Words

7. ____________ 7. they

8. ____________ 8. too

Name ______________________________

A. Read the words in the box. Then sort the words using the word endings.

hog	hop	hot	log	lot	top

Words with og	Words with ot	Words with op

B. Think of words that have the same word endings. Add them to the chart.

Name ____________________

A. Read the words in the box. Then sort the words using the word endings.

hop	hot	lot	top

Words with ot	**Words with op**

B. Think of words that have the same word endings. Add them to the chart.

Name ______________________________

A. Read the words in the box. Then sort the words using the word endings.

flop	hog	hop	hot	log	lot	slop	top

Words with <u>og</u>	**Words with <u>ot</u>**	**Words with <u>op</u>**

B. Think of words that have the same word endings. Add them to the chart.

Name ______________________________

hop	top	log	hog	hot
lot	flip	black	they	too

A. Write the spelling word that names the picture.

1. 

2. 

B. Circle the spelling word that completes the sentence.

3. They hop to the (hot, top).

4. We play a (log, lot).

5. I like to go, (too, black)!

6. Can you do a (they, flip)?

Name ______________________________

Trace and write O and o. Then copy the sentence. Make sure to leave spaces between words.

Oo

O O O O O O

O O O

o o o o o o o o o

o o o

Otto is outside.

Name ______________________________

The letters of the alphabet always stay in the same order.

a b c d e f g h i j k l m n o p q r s t u v w x y z

Read the words in the box. Underline the first letter of each word. Write the words in ABC order.

ant	glass	sit	jam

1. ______________________________

2. ______________________________

3. ______________________________

4. ______________________________

Name ______________________________

A. Read the words in the box out loud. Then write the words in ABC order.

wig	lock	fox

1. ______________________________

2. ______________________________

3. ______________________________

B. Choose one of the words from the box to write a sentence.

____

____

____

Name ______________________________

A. Read and spell each word in the box. Complete each sentence. Use one of the words in the box.

fun	make	they	too

1. ______________ like to jump.

2. Mom can jog, ______________.

3. It is ______________ to hop.

4. Dad can ______________ a cake.

B. Write your own sentence using a word from the box.

____

Teacher Directions: Point to the word *fun*. Use the Read/Spell/Write routine. Repeat for each word in the box.

Name ______________________________

An **exclamation** is a sentence that shows strong feelings.

It ends with an exclamation mark.

Example: Pal can run fast!

An interjection is an short exclamation that shows emotion.

Example: Wow!

Read each sentence. Add an exclamation mark to each exclamation or interjection.

1. Great ______________

2. He can kick ______________

3. Oh, no ______________

4. We're late ______________ .

Name ______________________________

A. Read the draft model. Find the errors.

Draft Model

wow

Mack can flip

hurray

B. Revise the draft by fixing the errors you found. Use exclamation marks correctly.

____

____

____

____

____

Connect to Writing

C. Look in your writer's notebook. Make sure you used exclamation marks correctly.

Name ______________________________

Exclamations and interjections end with exclamation marks.

Example: Yay! Don can win!

Write the correct end mark for each sentence on the line.

1. Oops ____________

2. She missed the goal ____________

3. Try again, Pam ____________

4. Good job ____________

5. She made the goal ____________

What Can It Do?

A cat can hop.

Teacher Directions: Have children establish a purpose for reading the take-home story.

1

A dog can jog.

Connect to Community: Have children talk to a family member about other animals they know.

4

A fox can nap.

②

An ox can pull.

③

Name ______________________________

Say each picture name and the sound that ends it. Circle the picture in each row whose name does NOT end with the same sound as the other two.

1.

2.

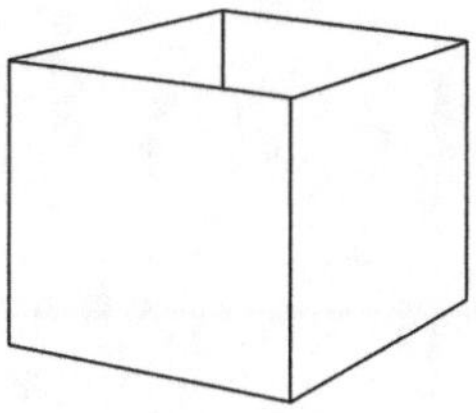

3.

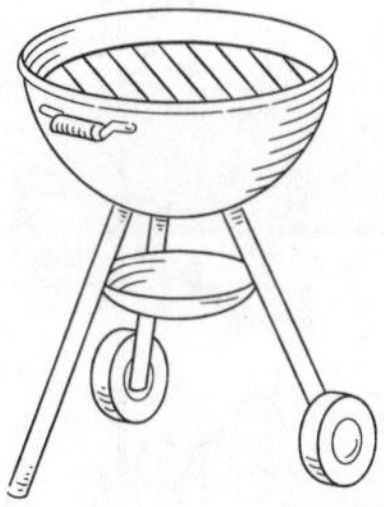

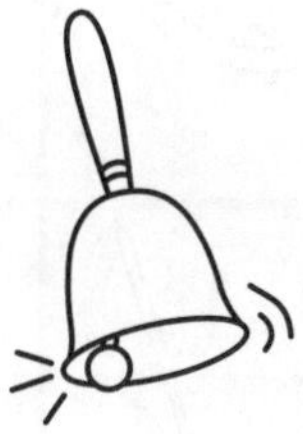

4.

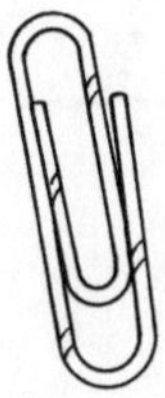

Teacher Directions: Model item 1 by saying *frog, hog,* and *doll.* Repeat, stressing the difference between the /g/ and /l/ ending sounds. Say: *The words* frog *and* hog *have the same ending sound: /g/.* Doll *has a different ending sound: /l/.* Guide children to circle the picture of the doll.

Name ______________________________

Say the name of each picture. Count the sounds. Then draw an X in one box for each sound.

1. 				
2. 				
3. 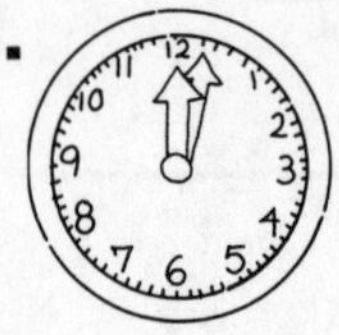				
4. 				
5. 				

Teacher Directions: Model item 1 by saying *dog.* Say: *I can say the sounds in the word dog. The word* dog *has three sounds: /d/ /o/ /g/. Say the sounds with me: /d/ /o/ /g/.*

Name ______________________________

Some words begin with a consonant blend. Listen to the beginning sounds in the word **crab**. You can hear the sound of each letter in the blend.

Read the word. Write the word. Circle the picture that it names.

1. frog

____

2. snap

____

3. crib

____

4. grass

____

Name ______________________________

A. Read each word that begins with a consonant blend. Write the word from the box that names each picture.

crib	grass	spin

1.  ______________________

2.  ______________________

3. 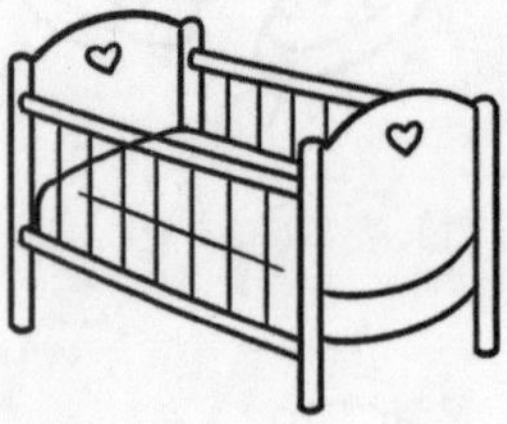 ______________________

B. Add one letter to make a new word with an r-blend or an s-blend. Then write the word.

1. dip ______________________ **2.** can ______________________

Name ______________________________

Fold back the paper along the dotted line. Use the blanks to write each word as it is read aloud. When you finish the test, unfold the paper. Use the list at the right to correct any spelling mistakes.

1. ____________	**1. spill**
2. ____________	**2. spin**
3. ____________	**3. grab**
4. ____________	**4. grass**
5. ____________	**5. drop**
6. ____________	**6. drip**
High-Frequency Words **7.** ____________	**7. two**
8. ____________	**8. move**

Name ______________________________

A. Read the words in the box. Then sort the words using the word blends.

spin	grass	grab	drop	spill	drip

Words with <u>dr</u>	Words with <u>sp</u>	Words with <u>gr</u>

B. Think of words that have the same word blends. Add them to the chart.

Name ______________________________

A. Read the words in the box. Then sort the words using the word blends.

drip	spill	drop	spin

Words with sp	Words with dr

B. Think of words that have the same word blends. Add them to the chart.

Name ________________________________

A. Read the words in the box. Then sort the words.

branch	drip	grab	spill
drop	grass	spin	stamp

Words with dr	**Words with br**	**Words with gr**
______	______	______
______	______	______
______	______	______

Words with st	**Words with sp**
______	______
______	______
______	______

B. Think of new words to add to the chart.

Name ____________________

spill	spin	grab	grass	drop
drip	hop	lot	two	move

Write the spelling word that names the picture.

1.

2.

3.

4.

5.

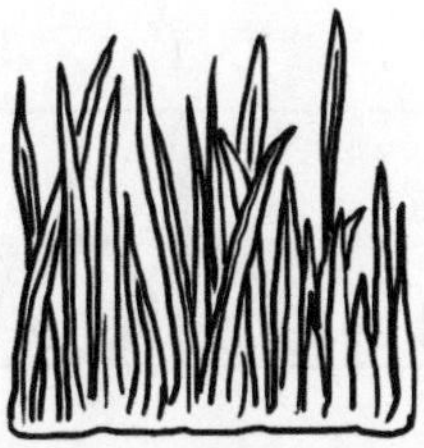

6.

Name ____________________

Trace and write <u>S</u> and <u>s</u>. Then copy the sentence. Make sure to leave spaces between words.

S S S S S S

S S S

s s s s s s s s

s s s

The snail slides slowly.

Name ______________________________

An **'s** at the end of a naming word means that something belongs to that person or thing.

Matt's hat

A. Underline the word that tells that something belongs to a person or thing. Write the word.

1. Dan's cat is little. ____________

2. This is my cat's mat. ____________

3. Pam's pals play. ____________

B. Write a sentence using a word with 's.

____

Name ___________________________

A. Circle the word that completes each sentence.

1. The (dogs, dog's) play.

2. The (girls, girl's) dress is pink.

3. The (birds, bird's) are in the tree.

4. The (boys, boy's) hat is red.

5. (Frans, Fran's) doll is on the bed.

B. Use one of the words you circled above to write a new sentence.

Name ______________________________

A. Read and spell each word in the box. Write the word from the box that completes each sentence.

jump	move	run	two

1. I can ________________. 

2. I ________________ a big box. 

3. I can ________________. 

4. I have ________________ cats. 

Teacher Directions: Point to the word *jump*. Use the Read/Spell/Write routine. Repeat for each word in the box.

Name ______________________________

A sentence is a group of words that tells a whole idea.

Every sentence begins with a capital letter and ends with a punctuation mark.

Write each sentence correctly.
Begin with a capital letter.
Add the mark shown in ( ).

1. I can help you (period)

____

2. can I play (question mark)

____

3. Look at Cass go up (exclamation mark)

____

Name ______________________________

A. Read the draft model. Find the errors.

Draft Model

Can she jupm
she can do it

B. Revise the draft. Make sure you capitalize the first word and use correct punctuation. Make sure to correct the spelling of high-frequency words.

____

____

____

____

Connect to Writing

C. Look in your writer's notebook. Make sure to capitalize the first word and use punctuation correctly. Make sure to correct the spelling of high-frequency words.

Name ________________________________

> Begin every sentence with a capital letter.
>
> End every sentence with a punctuation mark.

Unscramble the words in the box to complete each sentence. Write the sentence in order. Start with a capital letter and use the correct mark at the end.

1. Nat | swim can here |

____

2. did | have fun Nat |

____

3. look | Nat at go |

____

We are kids.

We can move.

We can have fun!

Connect to Community: Have children talk to a family member about ways they can move.

4

Kids Can Move

He can hop.

Teacher Directions: Have children establish a purpose for reading the take-home story.

1

She can run fast.

②

They can jump.

③

Name ______________________________

Listen to the sounds your teacher says. Blend the sounds together. Draw a picture of the word you made.

1.	**2.**
3.	**4.**

Teacher Directions: Model item 1 by saying */m/ /o/ /p/. Listen as I blend the sounds together: /mmmooop/, mop.* Model drawing a mop in the first box and have children copy. For items 2–4, have children listen to the sounds and blend them to form a word. 2. Say: /g/ /l/ /a/ /s/; 3. Say: /d/ /r/ /e/ /s/; 4. Say: /b/ /r/ /e/ /d/.

Name ______________________________

Say each picture name. Say the middle sounds. Circle the picture whose name has the same middle sound as the first picture in the row.

1.			
2.			
3.	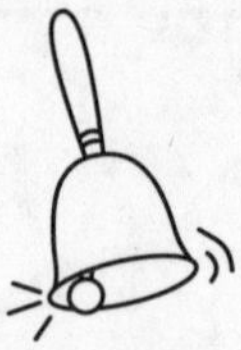		
4.	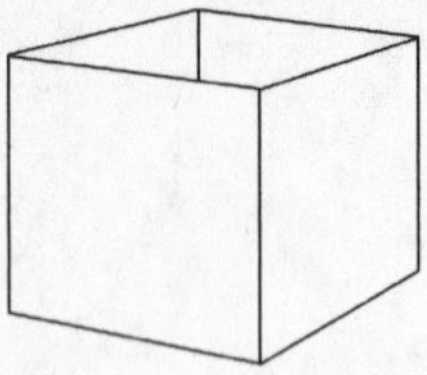		
5.			

Teacher Directions: Model item 1 by saying /p/ /i/ /g/. Emphasize the middle sound. Then say *six* and *mop* and explicitly compare middle sounds. Say: *The words* pig *and* six *have the same middle sound: /i/.* Mop *has a different middle sound: /o/.* Guide children to circle the picture of the number six.

Name ______________________________

The letters **e** or **ea** can make the short **e** sound.

leg  **bread** 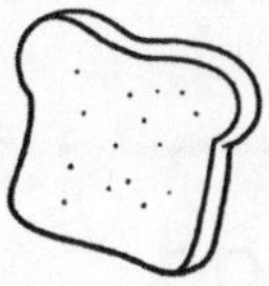

A. Read the words in the box. Listen for the short e sound. Write the word that names each picture.

bed	vet	head	men

1. ______________ 

2. ______________ 

3. ______________ 

4. ______________ 

B. Write a sentence using a word from the box.

____

____

____

Name ______________________________

A. Read the words in the box. Use a word in the box to complete each sentence.

dress	bread	ten	pet	egg	head

I. Ben has ______________ hats.

2. Dan will have ______________.

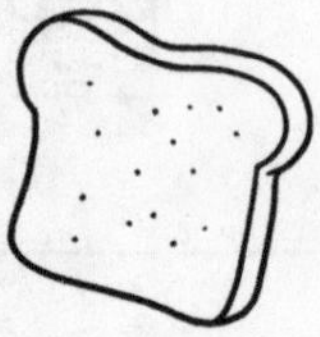

3. This nest has an ______________.

4. Max is a good ______________.

B. Change one letter to make a new word with the short e sound. Then write the word.

I. man ______________ 2. pat ______________

Name ______________________________

Fold back the paper along the dotted line. Use the blanks to write each word as it is read aloud. When you finish the test, unfold the paper. Use the list at the right to correct any spelling mistakes.

1. ____________	1. leg
2. ____________	2. beg
3. ____________	3. men
4. ____________	4. hen
5. ____________	5. head
6. ____________	6. bread

High-Frequency Words

7. ____________	7. there
8. ____________	8. again

Name ______________________________

A. Read the words in the box. Say each word. Then sort the words.

beg	bread	head	hen	leg	men

Words with ead	Words with en	Words with eg

B. Think of some new words with the same endings. Add words to your chart.

Name ____________________

A. Read the words in the box. Say each word. Then sort the words.

head	hen	men	read

Words with <u>ead</u>	Words with <u>en</u>
______________	______________
______________	______________
______________	______________
______________	______________

B. Think of some new words with the same endings. Add words to your chart.

Name ______________________________

A. Read the words in the box. Then sort the words.

beg	bread	head	hen	leg	men	sled	spread

Words with ead	**Words with en**
______	______
______	______
______	______
______	______
______	______
Words with eg	**Words with ed**
______	______
______	______
______	______

B. Think of some new words. Add words to your chart.

Name ______________________

Read each word in the box. Say each word.

leg	beg	men	hen
read	grass	spill	again

Use the clues to write a spelling word on the line.

1. starts like **miss** + ends like **ten** ______________

2. starts like **back** + ends like **peg** ______________

3. starts like **hat** + ends like **ten** ______________

4. starts like **rock** + ends like **head** ______________

5. starts like **spin** + ends like **hill** ______________

Name ______________________________

Trace and write E and e. Then copy the sentence. Make sure to leave spaces between words.

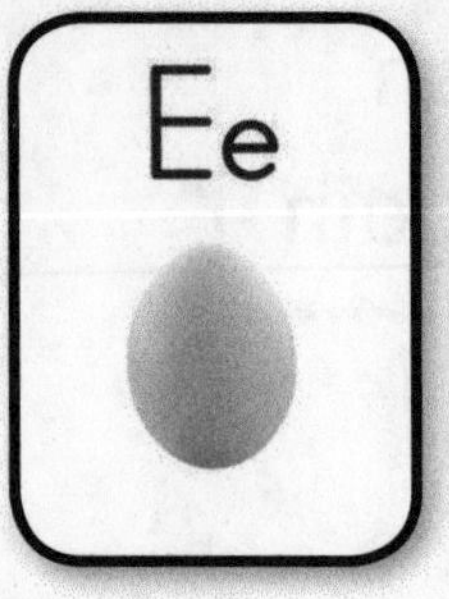

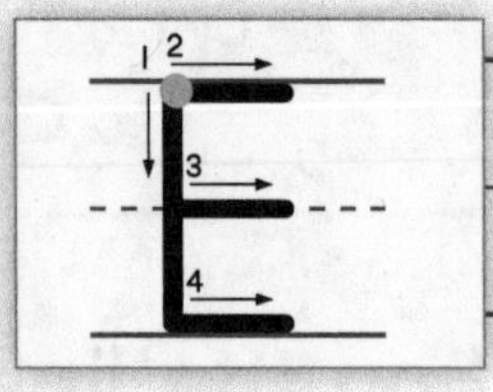

E E E E

E E E

e e e e e e

e e e

Ed and Ellen eat.

Name ______________________________

Add the ending **-ed** to an action word to tell about something that already happened. The ending **-ed** can make different sounds. Read the words. Listen for the different sounds at the end of **helped** and **filled**.

help **helped** **fill** **filled**

A. Add -ed to each word. Write and say each word.

1. dress + ed = ______________________

2. mix + ed = ______________________

3. spill + ed = ______________________

B. Use a word you wrote above to write a new sentence.

____

Name ___________________________________

A. Read the words in ( ). Circle the word that completes each sentence.

1. The snake (hissd, hissed).

2. I (miss, missed) the bus yesterday.

3. Chad (filled, filld) his cup.

4. Jess (toss, tossed) the ball.

5. She (spelled, spell) her name.

6. Dan (help, helped) me fix the clock.

B. Use one of the words you circled above to write a new sentence.

____

____

Name ______________________________

A. Read and spell each word in the box. Complete each sentence using a word in the box.

again	help	new	there	use

1. My cat is up ____________________.

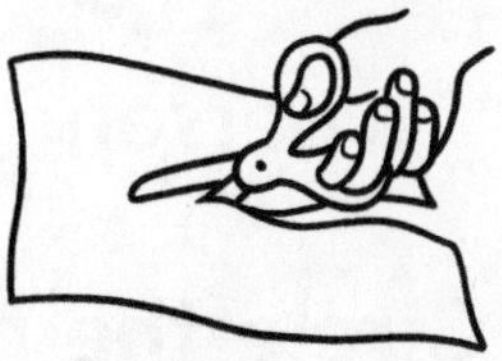

2. We can ____________________ this.

3. This hat is ____________________.

4. Ken will ____________________ me.

5. Ned will try ____________________.

B. Write your own sentence using a word from the box.

____

____

Name ____________________

A **noun** names a person, place, or thing.

A. Say the name of the noun in the picture.

person

place

thing

B. Circle the noun in each sentence.

1. The van is big.

2. A pet swims.

3. Miss Kim has a book.

4. We are at school.

5. A man helps us cross.

Name ______________________________

A. Read the draft model. Circle the nouns.

Draft Model

A dog plays.

The boy runs.

B. Now revise the draft by adding new words to the sentences. Rewrite the sentences below.

____

____

____

____

Connect to Writing

C. Look in your writer's notebook. Circle the nouns in your sentences. Fix any errors.

Name ______________________________

In a list with three or more nouns, a comma is used after all but the last noun.

A noun names a person, place, or thing.

Example: Frogs, cats, and dogs are in the pet show.

Write the statement correctly.

1. Nick sells beds cribs and clocks.

____

2. Mel has his sled hat and bag.

____

3. Mom Dad Jim and Ann like bugs.

____

4. A truck bus and cab can go.

____

They fix the clock.
Ben is glad!

Connect to Community: Have children talk to a family member about times they have helped at home.

4

A Fun Job

A clock can stop.
Mom can fix it!

Teacher Directions: Have children establish a purpose for reading the take-home story.

1

Ben helps his mom.
Ben likes his job.

②

Dad helps, too.
Can they fix the clock?

③

Name ____

Words that rhyme end in the same sounds.

Say each picture name. Then draw a picture of something whose name rhymes with it.

1. 	
2. 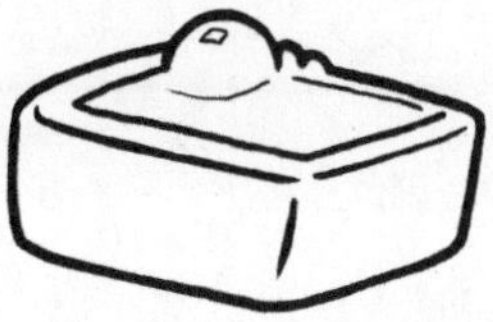	
3. 	
4. 	
5. 	

Teacher Directions: Read the box at the top of the page aloud. Point to the pictures as you say each word: *pup, cup.* Point out that these words rhyme.

Name ______________________________

Listen to the sounds your teacher says. Put them together. Circle the picture that goes with the word you made.

1.

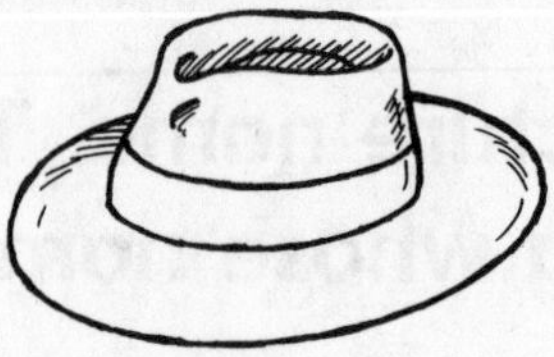

2.

3.

4.

5.

Teacher Directions: Model item 1 by saying /h/ /u/ /t/. *I will blend the sounds to make a word: /huuut/, hut.* Guide children to circle the picture of the hut for item 1. For items 2–5, say the following sounds. Have children blend the sounds to say each word. Then have them circle the picture that shows it. 2. /s/ /u/ /n/; 3. /p/ /u/ /p/; 4. /t/ /r/ /u/ /k/; 5. /d/ /r/ /u/ /m/.

Name ______________________________

The letter u can make the short **u** sound you hear in **rug**.

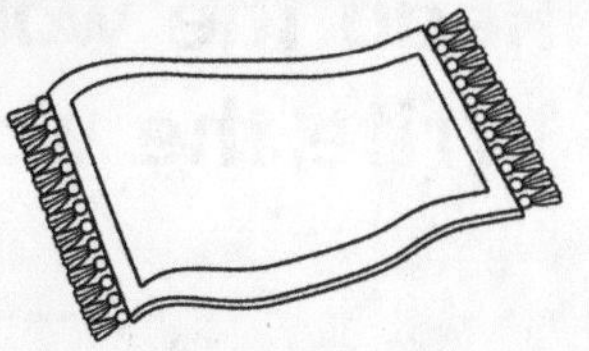

Read the words in the box out loud. Write a word from the box to describe each picture.

sun	bus	up	drum	mud

1.  ______________________

2.  ______________________

3.  ______________________

4.  ______________________

Name ______________________________

A. Read the words. Listen for the short u sound. Write the word that names each picture.

cut	bug	hut	duck	pup

1. ____________ 

2. ____________ 

3. ____________ 

4. ____________ 

B. Change one letter to make a new word with the short u sound. Then write the word.

1. not ____________

2. ran ____________

3. bag ____________

4. fan ____________

Name ______________________________

Fold back the paper along the dotted line. Use the blanks to write each word as it is read aloud. When you finish the test, unfold the paper. Use the list at the right to correct any spelling mistakes.

1. ______________ **1. run**

2. ______________ **2. fun**

3. ______________ **3. nut**

4. ______________ **4. cut**

5. ______________ **5. bug**

6. ______________ **6. rug**

High-Frequency Words

7. ______________ **7. could**

8. ______________ **8. one**

Name ______________________________

A. Read the words in the box out loud. Then sort the words.

cut   run   nut   fun   bug   rug

Words with un	**Words with ut**	**Words with ug**

B. Think of some new words. Add words to your chart.

Name ______________________________

A. Read the words in the box out loud. Then sort the words.

bug	fun	rug	run

Words with ug	Words with un

B. Think of some new words. Add words to your chart.

Name ______________________________

A. Read the words in the box out loud. Then sort the words.

bug cut fun lunch nut rug run skunk

Words with un	Words with ut	Words with ug

B. Think of some new words. Add words to your chart.

Name ______________________________

fun	rug	bed	run	head	bug

A. Write the spelling word that completes the sentence.

1. The ______________ can fly.

2. We have ______________ when we play.

3. He can ______________ so fast.

4. She sat on the ______________ .

B. Write the word that names the picture.

1. 

2. 

Name ______________________________

Trace and write U and u. Then copy the sentence. Make sure to leave spaces between words.

Uu

U U U U

U U U

u u u u u u

u u u

Un is upstairs.

Name ______________________________

A **contraction** is when you put two words together to make one word. Read the words: **he is.** Now read the contraction: **he’s.**

The apostrophe (’) stands for the missing letter i in is.

A. Read the two words. Write and read the contraction.

1. she is ____________ 2. he is ____________

3. it is ____________ 4. let us ____________

B. Read the sentences out loud. Circle the contractions.

1. Let’s go to the store.

2. Do you know if it’s cold out?

3. She’s bringing her coat.

Name ______________________________

A. Read the contractions. Write the two words that make up the contraction.

1. it's = ______________

2. let's = ______________

3. she's = ______________

B. Use a contraction from the box to complete the sentences. Then read the sentences out loud.

it's	he's	she's

1. ______________ reading a story.

2. ______________ his new favorite book.

3. ______________ playing ball.

Name ____________________

Read the words in the box out loud. Complete each sentence. Use one of the words in the box.

three	could	live	one	then

1. I ____________ in the city.

2. There is ____________ duck.

3. Sam ____________ swim.

4. She has ____________ pups.

5. I run up the hill.

____

____________ I run down the hill.

Name ________________________________

A **singular noun** names one person, one place, or one thing.

A **plural noun** names more than one person, place, or thing.

If a noun ends in **-x**, -s, or **-ss**, add **-es** to make it plural. Example: **one fox two foxes**

Read the singular nouns in the box. Then write a plural noun to complete the sentences.

bus	box	glass	dress

1. The ____________ stop here.

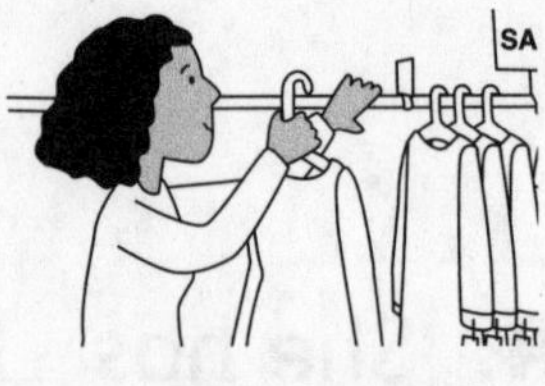

2. Lin will hang the ____________ up.

3. Nick has ____________ in his truck.

4. Pat will set up the ____________ .

Name ______________________________

A. Read the draft. Find the errors in singular and plural nouns.

Draft Model

The truck are stuck in mud.
There are box in the trucks.

B. Revise the draft by fixing the errors. Make sure you use singular and plural nouns correctly.

____

____

____

Connect to Writing

C. Look in your writer's notebook. Circle the nouns you used. Make sure you used singular and plural nouns correctly.

Name ________________________________

A **contraction** is a shorter way of writing two words.

Example: it is → it's

In the example, the apostrophe (') replaces the letter i.

Write the contraction for the underlined words in each sentence. Read the sentences aloud.

1. Where is the box? ____________

2. He is getting six eggs. ____________

3. She is putting eggs in the boxes. ____________

4. There is a big truck. ____________

Cub plays a jug.

The pals have fun!

Connect to Community: Have children talk to a family member about instruments they know.

Pals Play and Hum

Look at Bug.

Bug can hum.

Teacher Directions: Have children establish a purpose for reading the take-home story.

Look at Duck!
Duck can pluck.

2

Do you see Frog?
Frog can drum.

3

Name ______________________________

Listen to the sounds your teacher says. Blend the sounds together to make a word. Circle the picture that matches the word you made.

1.

2.

3.

4.

5.

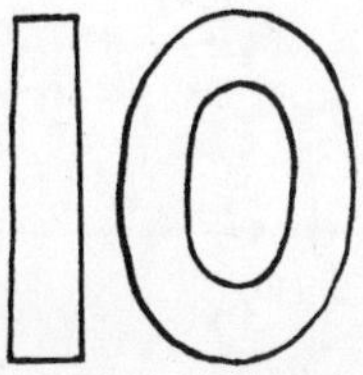

Teacher Directions: 1. Model: *When we say the word* skunk, *we blend the sounds of the letters* s *and* k *together: /sk/. We also blend the sounds of the letters* n *and* k: */nk/. Listen as I blend the sounds to say the word: /s/ /k/ /u/ /n/ /k/, skunk.* 2. Say: /p/ /o/ /n/ /d/, pond; 3. Say: /n/ /e/ /s/ /t/, nest; 4. Say: /s/ /i/ /n/ /k/, sink; 5. Say: /s/ /t/ /a/ /m/ /p/, stamp.

Name ______________________________

Listen to the sounds your teacher says. Blend the sounds together. Draw a picture of the word you made.

1.	**2.**
3.	**4.**

Teacher Directions: Model item 1 by saying */h/ /a/ /n/ /d/. Listen as I blend these sounds: /hhhaaannnd/, hand.* Model drawing a hand in the first box and have children copy. For items 2–4, have children listen to the sounds and blend them to form a word. 2. Say: /p/ /o/ /n/ /d/; 3. Say: /a/ /n/ /t/; 4. Say: /j/ /u/ /m/ /p/.

Name ____

Some words have end blends, such as **st** and **nk**. The letters **st** make the ending sounds in **nest**. The letters **nk** make the ending sounds in **sink**.

nest  **sink** 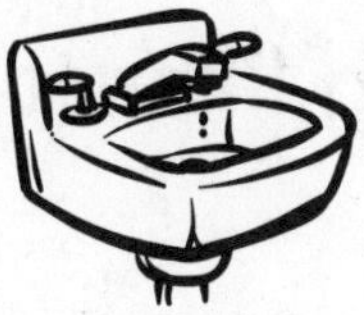

Read the words in the box. Listen for the end blend. Write the word that names each picture. Underline the end blend.

list	hand	tent	bank	desk	lamp

1. ____________________ 

2. ____________________ 

3. ____________________ 

4. ____________________ 

5. ____________________ 

6. ____________________ 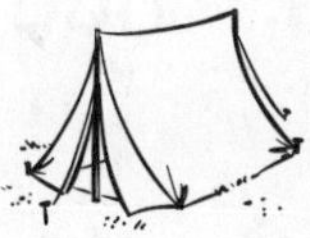

Name ______________________________

A. Read each sentence. Underline a word that has an end blend. Write the word.

1. My dog likes to jump up. ____________

2. Pam did the best job. ____________

3. Bob will send a box to Jan. ____________

4. Set the cup in the sink. ____________

B. Add one letter to make a new word with an n-blend. Then write the word.

1. had ____________

2. bed ____________

Name ______________________________

Fold back the paper along the dotted line. Use the blanks to write each word as it is read aloud. When you finish the test, unfold the paper. Use the list at the right to correct any spelling mistakes.

1. ______________ **1. lend**

2. ______________ **2. send**

3. ______________ **3. fast**

4. ______________ **4. past**

5. ______________ **5. sink**

6. ______________ **6. wink**

High-Frequency Words

7. ______________ **7. of**

8. ______________ **8. who**

Name ______________________________

A. Read the words in the box. Say each word. Then sort the words.

fast	lend	past	sink	send	wink

Words with nd	Words with st	Words with nk

B. Think of some new words. Add words to your chart.

Name ______________________________

A. Read the words in the box. Say each word. Then sort the words.

fast	lend	past	send

Words with nd	**Words with st**
______________	______________
______________	______________
______________	______________

B. Think of some new words. Add words to your chart.

Name ____________________

A. Read the words in the box. Then sort the words.

fast left lend past send sink twist wink

Words with <u>ft</u>	**Words with <u>st</u>**

Words with <u>nd</u>	**Words with <u>nk</u>**

B. Think of some new words. Add words to your chart.

Name ______________________

lend	send	fast	past	sink
wink	run	bug	of	who

A. Write the spelling word that names the picture.

1. ______________________

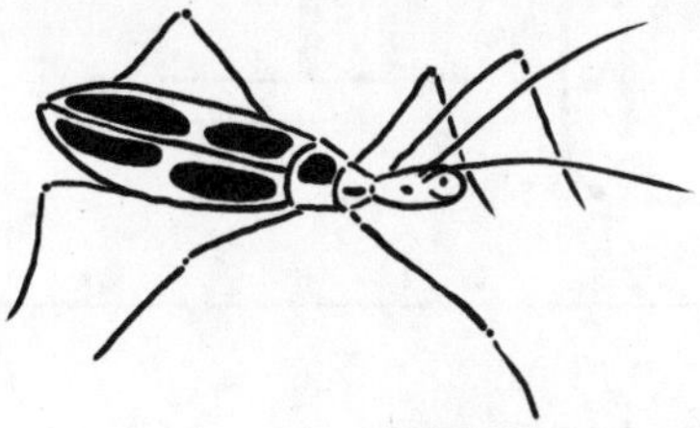

2. ______________________

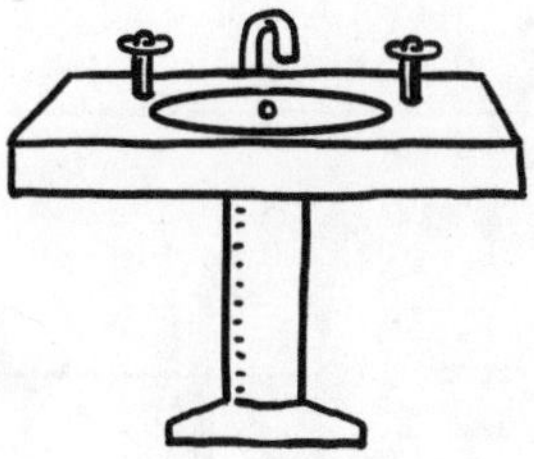

B. Write the spelling word that completes the sentence.

3. I can ____________ you a kiss.

4. Can you ____________ ?

5. This cat can ____________ !

Name ______________________________

Trace and write T and t. Then copy the sentence. Make sure to leave spaces between words.

T T T T T T

T

t t t t t t t t

t

Tom has the tent.

Name ______________________________

Add the ending -ing to an action word to tell what is happening now.

jump **jumping**

A. Add -ing to each word. Write the new word.

1. pack + ing = ______________

2. help + ing = ______________

3. ask + ing = ______________

B. Use a word you wrote above to complete the sentence.

4. She is ______________ a bag.

Name ______________________________

A. Circle the word that completes each sentence.

1. Jen is (stacks, stacking) bricks.

2. The cars are (honking, honk).

3. Russ is (plants, planting).

4. My dog Lex (rests, resting) in his bed.

5. Dad (camping, camps) with Ben in a tent.

B. Use one of the words you circled above to write a new sentence.

____

____

Name ______________________________

A. Use the words in the box to complete each sentence.

eat	no	of	under	who

I. ______________ can help Dan?

2. We have ______________ lamp.

3. The cat is ______________ the desk.

4. Bats ______________ bugs.

5. His hands are full ______________ mud.

B. Write your own sentence using a word from the box.

____

____

Name ________________________________

A **possessive noun** tells who or what has something. A possessive noun that tells about one person or thing ends with **'s**. A possessive noun that tells about more than one person or thing ends with **s'**.

Examples: a dog's hut, the girls' books

A. Circle the possessive noun in each sentence.

1. The ants' hill is big.
2. The pigs' pen is a mess.
3. My pal's pet is little.
4. My mom's hat is red.

B. Write your own sentence. Use one of the possessive nouns you circled.

____

____

____

Name ______________________________

A. Read the draft model. Circle the errors.

Draft Model

The girls tents are big.

The dogs bed is little.

B. Now revise the draft by fixing the errors you found. Make sure you use possessive nouns correctly.

____

____

____

____

Connect to Writing

C. Look in your writer's notebook. Fix any errors in your sentences. Check that you used possessive nouns correctly.

Name ______________________________

A possessive noun that tells about one person or thing ends with **'s**. A possessive noun that tells about more than one person or thing ends with **s'**.

Write each sentence correctly.

1. The ants hill is little.

____

2. A skunks smell is bad.

____

3. The kids school is big.

____

4. A pigs' pal is a duck.

____

Big Rock Pond

This is Big Rock Pond.
What can we see?

Teacher Directions: Have children establish a purpose for reading the take-home story.

Here are three bats.
Three bats spin.

Connect to Community: Have children talk to a family member about their favorite animals.

Here is one bug.
A bug can buzz and buzz.

②

Here are two frogs.
Two frogs jump.

③

Name ______________________________

Say each picture name. Say the middle sounds. Circle the picture whose name has the same middle sound as the first picture in the row.

Teacher Directions: Model item 1 by saying /s/ /i/ /ks/. Emphasize the middle sound. Then say *fish* and *sack* and explicitly compare middle sounds. Say: *The words* six *and* fish *have the same middle sound: /i/.* Sack *has a different middle sound: /a/.* Guide children to circle the picture of the fish.

Name ______________________________

Say each picture name and the sound that begins it. Circle the picture in each row whose name does NOT begin with the same sound as the other two.

1.

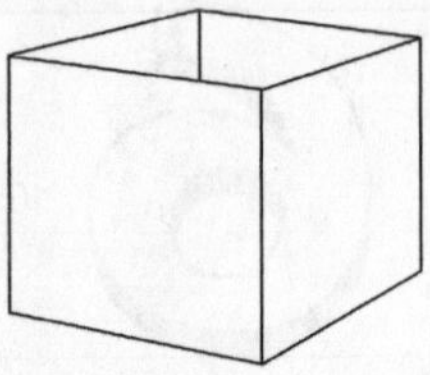

2.

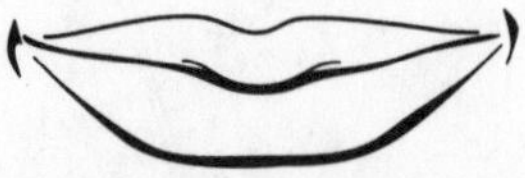

3.

4.

5.

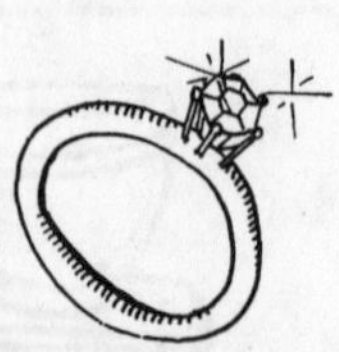

Teacher Directions: Model item 1 by saying *bat, hat,* and *box*. Repeat, stressing the difference between the /b/ and /h/ beginning sounds. Say: *The words bat and box have the same beginning sound: /b/.* Hat *has a different beginning sound: /h/.* Guide children to circle the picture of the hat.

Name ______________________________

The letters **sh** make the ending sound in **fish**.
The letters **th** make the beginning sound in **thin**.
The letters **ng** make the ending sound in **ring**.

Read each sentence. Circle the word that has sh th, or ng. Write the word.

1. Here is a fresh plum. ____________________

2. Min and Dan like to sing. ____________________

3. Say thank you for a gift. ____________________

4. Sam and Dad pick up shells. ____________________

5. I like to play with my pals. ____________________

Name ______________________________

A. Read the words in the box. Write the word that names each picture.

bath	swings	think	path

1.

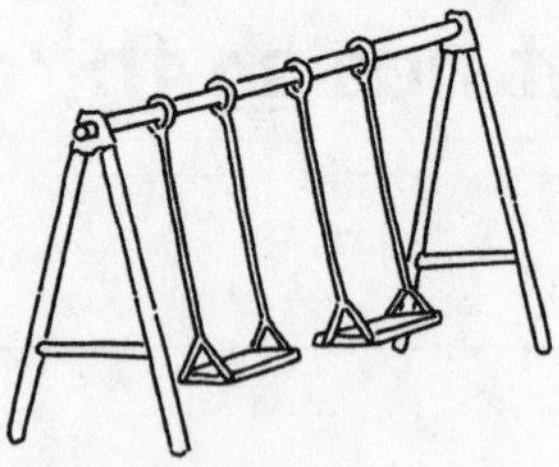

2.

3.

4.

B. Add one letter to make a new word with the ending sound you hear in swing.

1. ran ______________ **2.** win ______________

Name ______________________________

Fold back the paper along the dotted line. Use the blanks to write each word as it is read aloud. When you finish the test, unfold the paper. Use the list at the right to correct any spelling mistakes.

1. ______________ **1. fish**

2. ______________ **2. shop**

3. ______________ **3. ship**

4. ______________ **4. with**

5. ______________ **5. thing**

6. ______________ **6. sang**

High-Frequency Words

7. ______________ **7. want**

8. ______________ **8. call**

Name ______________________________

A. Read the words in the box. Then sort the words.

with sang ship shop thing fish

Words with <u>sh</u>	Words with <u>th</u>	Words with <u>ng</u>

B. Think of new words to add to the chart.

Name ______________________________

A. Read the words in the box. Then sort the words.

ship	sing	shop	with

Words with <u>sh</u>	Words with <u>th</u>	Words with <u>ng</u>
________	________	________
________	________	________
________	________	________

B. Think of new words to add to the chart.

Name ______________________________

A. Read the words in the box. Then sort the words.

fish	sang	ship	shop	sixth	thick	thing	with

Words with sh	Words with th	Words with ng

B. Think of new words to add to the chart.

Name ______________________________

Use the clues to write a word from the box on the line.

fish	shop	ship	with	thing
sang	fast	wink	want	call

1. starts like **shell** + ends like **hop** ______________

2. starts like **them** + ends like **sing** ______________

3. starts like **fin** + ends like **last** ______________

4. starts like **sit** + ends like **hang** ______________

5. starts like **win** + ends like **sink** ______________

6. starts like **fan** + ends like **wish** ______________

Name ______________________________

Trace and write F and f. Then copy the sentence. Make sure to leave spaces between words.

Ff

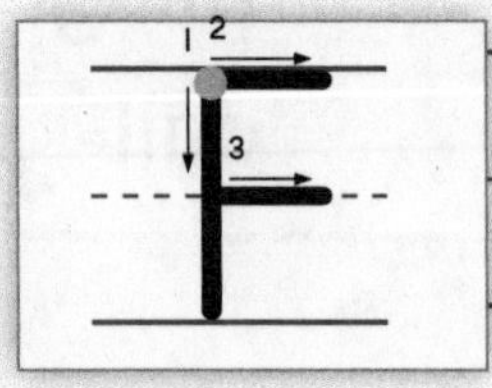

F F F F F

F

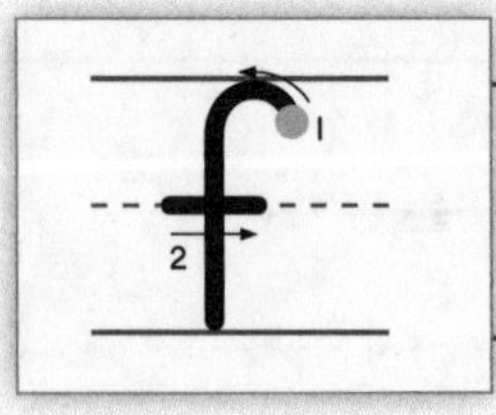

f f f f f f f f

f

Fred flies the flag.

Name ______________________________

When a syllable ends in a consonant and has one vowel letter, the vowel sound is usually short. This is called a **closed syllable**.

rab/bit   bas/ket   cab/in

Read each word. Draw a line between the syllables. Write each syllable on a line.

1. finish ____________ ____________

2. pumpkin ____________ ____________

3. napkin ____________ ____________

4. locket ____________ ____________

Name ______________________________

A. Read each word. Draw a line between the syllables.

1. basket ______ ______

2. helping ______ ______

3. jumping ______ ______

4. magnet ______ ______

5. rabbit ______ ______

B. Use one of the words from above to write a sentence.

____

____

Name ______________________________

Read each sentence out loud. Match each sentence to the picture.

1. I **want** that one. a. 

2. We **all** have a snack. b. 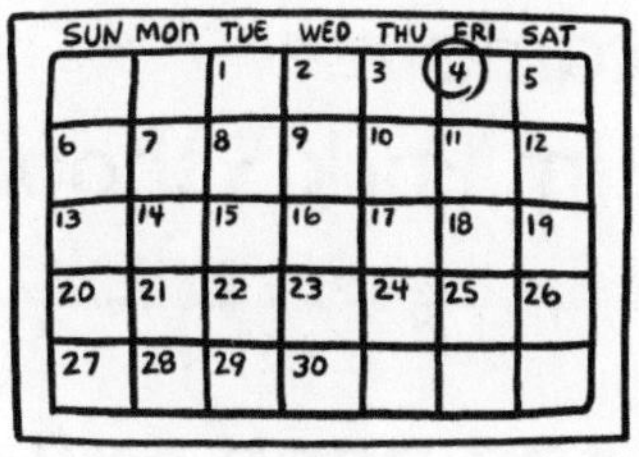

3. What **day** is this? c. 

4. **Her** socks have dots. d. 

5. I use this to **call** Dad. e. 

Name ______________________________

Common nouns name general people, places, or things. A common noun begins with a lowercase letter.

Example:
girl

Proper nouns name specific people, places, or things. A proper noun begins with a capital letter.

Example:
Elm Park School

A. Read each row of words. Circle the word or words that are proper nouns. Make an X on the common nouns.

1.	Kim	dog	hand
2.	girl	Nan	cat
3.	swing	Pine Park	Miss Miller
4.	Bob	Ed	Elm Street

B. Complete the sentence. Use one of the proper nouns circled.

5. ______________ and ______________ go to ______________.

Name ____________________

A. Read the draft. Circle the errors in common and proper nouns.

Draft Model

miss lane teaches at rock hill school.

Our School is on pine street.

B. Now revise the draft by fixing the errors you found. Remember to capitalize proper nouns.

Connect to Writing

C. Look in your writer's notebook. Make sure you capitalized proper nouns. Check capitalization for common nouns.

Name ______________________________

A proper noun begins with a capital letter.

Write each proper noun correctly on the lines.

1. nick is up. ______________

2. My pet cat is called seth. ______________

3. I will ask greg to help me. ______________

4. We have fun at frog pond. ______________

5. I go to camp playland. ______________

All the dogs help.

They see the play!

Connect to Community: Have children talk to a family member about a time they helped a friend.

All Help with the Play

Let's have a play.

We can all help.

Teacher Directions: Have children establish a purpose for reading the take-home story.

Rex makes fun hats.
Shep makes tops with dots.

(2)

What can we do?
We want to help.

(3)

Name ____________________

Say the name of each picture. Count the sounds in each word. Then draw an X in one box for each sound.

1. 				
2. 				
3. 				
4. 				
5. 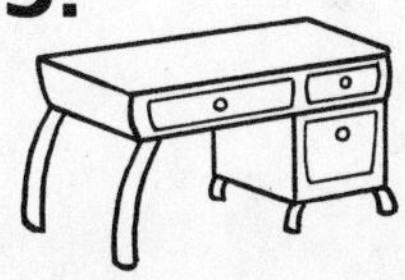				

Teacher Directions: Model item 1 by saying *nest*. Say: *I can say the sounds in the word* nest. *The word* nest *has four sounds: /n/ /e/ /s/ /t/. Say the sounds with me: /n/ /e/ /s/ /t/.* Guide children to draw four X's for item 1.

Name ____

Listen to each word your teacher says. Add the beginning sound. Circle the picture of the new word you made.

1.

2.

3.

4.

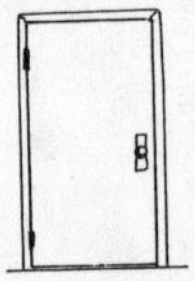

5.

Teacher Directions: 1. Model: *I can add sounds to words to make new words. Listen to the word:* ox. *I can add the /f/ sound to the beginning of* ox *to make the new word /foks/. Say the new word with me:* fox. 2. Say *at.* Tell children to add /h/ to the beginning of *at.* 3. Say *up.* Tell children to add /p/ to the beginning of *up.* 4. Say *or.* Tell children to add /d/ to the beginning of *or.* 5. Say *in.* Tell children to add /ch/ to the beginning of *in.*

Name ______________________________

The letters <u>**ch**</u> and <u>**tch**</u> stand for the sound you hear at the beginning of **<u>ch</u>ip** and the end of **di<u>tch</u>**. The letters <u>**wh**</u> stand for the sound at the beginning of **<u>wh</u>en**. The letters <u>**ph**</u> stand for the sound at the end of **gra<u>ph</u>**.

Read the words in the box. Match each word with a sound-spelling below. Write the word.

whisk	chin	Phil	graph
pitch	lunch	when	catch

1. wh ______________ ______________

2. ch ______________ ______________

3. ph ______________ ______________

4. tch ______________ ______________

Name ______________________________

A. Read the sentences out loud. Circle the word with wh, tch, or ph. Then write and read the word.

I. We like when we go to the park. ____________

2. Which game will we play? ____________

3. Phil will pick the game. ____________

4. I can catch the ball! ____________

B. Add letters to make a new word with the ending sound you hear in catch. Then write the word.

I. hut ____________ 2. pat ____________

Name ______________________________

Fold back the paper along the dotted line. Use the blanks to write each word as it is read aloud. When you finish the test, unfold the paper. Use the list at the right to correct any spelling mistakes.

1. ________ 1. whip
2. ________ 2. whale
3. ________ 3. catch
4. ________ 4. match
5. ________ 5. chin
6. ________ 6. graph

High-Frequency Words

7. ________ 7. many
8. ________ 8. around

Name ______________________________

A. Read the words in the box. Then sort the words.

catch	whale	chin	graph	match	whip

Words with ph	**Words with tch**
____________	____________
____________	____________
____________	____________

Words with ch	**Words with wh**
____________	____________
____________	____________
____________	____________

B. Think of words to add to the chart.

Name ____________________

A. Read the words in the box. Then sort the words.

catch	chin	graph	whale

Words with ph	Words with tch

Words with ch	Words with wh

B. Think of new words to add to the chart.

Name ______________________________

A. Read the words in the box. Then sort the words.

catch	chin	chop	graph
match	phone	whale	whip

Words with ph	Words with tch

Words with ch	Words with wh

B. Think of new words to add to the chart.

Name ______________________________

A. Read the words in the box.

whip	whale	catch	match	chin
graph	shop	path	many	around

B. Use the clues to write a spelling word on the line.

1. starts like **can** + ends like **batch** ____________

2. starts like **she** + ends like **mop** ____________

3. starts like **when** + ends like **hip** ____________

4. starts like **pup** + ends like **math** ____________

5. starts like **chip** + ends like **win** ____________

Name ____________________

Trace and write C and c. Then copy the sentence.
Make sure to leave spaces between words.

Cc

C C C C C C

C C C

c c c c c c c c

c c c

Chad can chat.

Name ______________________________

Add the ending -**es** to naming words that end in **ss**, **z**, **x**, **sh**, and **ch** to make them mean "more than one."

dish + es = dishes

A. Add -es to make the word mean "more than one."

1. dress ______________________

2. brush ______________________

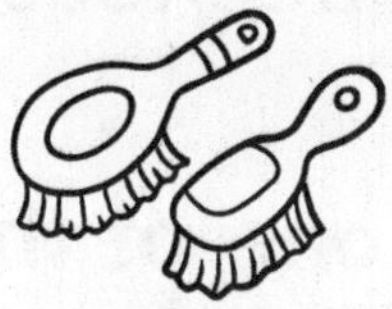

3. peach ______________________

4. box ______________________

B. Circle the word that means "more than one."

5. glass glasses

6. foxes fox

Name ______________________________

A. Circle the word that completes each sentence.

1. Dad has a lot of (dish, dishes).

2. The truck is filled with many (boxes, boxs).

3. Mom has one (dresses, dress).

4. Chad and Chuck sit on (benches, benchs).

5. The bee (buzzs, buzzes) by the flowers.

B. Use one of the words you circled above to write a new sentence.

____

____

Name ______________________________

A. Complete each sentence with a word from the box.

walk	many	by	place	around

1. This is a good ______________ to eat.

2. Ed will ______________ fast.

3. Ned sits ______________ the tree.

4. She has ______________ socks.

5. We go ______________ the rock.

B. Write your own sentence using a word from the box.

____

____

Name ____

Irregular plural nouns use new words to name more than one. They do not end in -**s** or -**es**.

A. Say the nouns and their plurals.

child

children

man

men

mouse

mice

foot
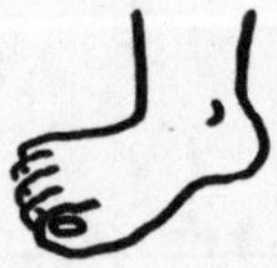
feet
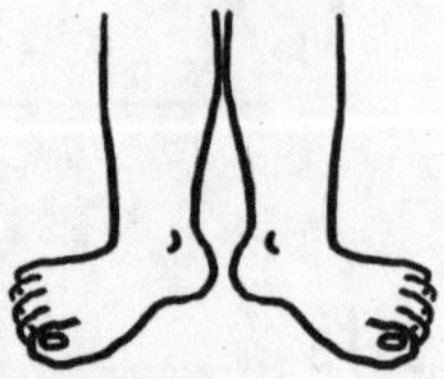

B. Write an irregular plural noun from above to complete each sentence.

1. The ______________________ can run in the bushes.

2. Three ______________________ swing up and down.

Name ______________________________

A. Read the draft model. Circle the errors.

Draft Model

Three mouse run and run.

They have little foot.

B. Revise the draft by fixing the errors you found. Make sure to use irregular plural nouns correctly.

____

____

____

____

Connect to Writing

C. Look in your writer's notebook. Make sure you used irregular plural nouns correctly.

Name ______________________________

> A sentence begins with a capital letter.
> A statement ends with a period.

Write each sentence correctly.

1. the dogs are in a show

____

2. one dog makes a mess?

____

3. The childs can have fun

____

4. that dog can jump

____

Look Around

Look around this place.
Some chicks hatch.

Teacher Directions: Have children establish a purpose for reading the take-home story.

Look around this place.
Many dogs fetch.

Connect to Community: Have children talk to a family member about a place they like to go and things that they see there.

Look around this place.
Many kids play catch.

Look around this place.
Lots of buses whiz by.

Name ______________________________

Listen to the sounds your teacher says. Blend the sounds together. Circle the picture that goes with the word you made.

1.

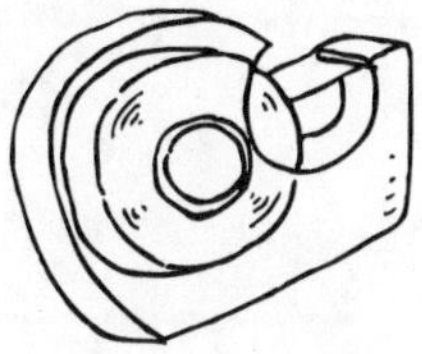

2.

3.

4.

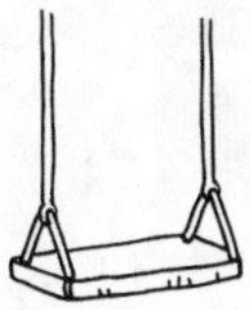

5.

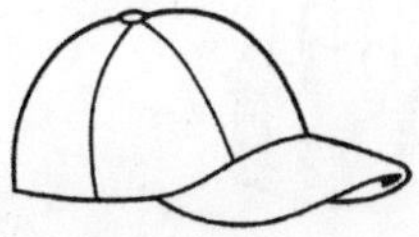

Teacher Directions: Model item 1 by saying: /ā/ /p/. *I will blend the sounds to make a word: /āāāp/, ape.* Guide children to circle the picture of the ape for item 1. For items 2–5, say the following sounds. Have students blend the sounds to say each word. Then have them circle the picture that shows it. 2. /k/ /ā/ /k/; 3. /ch/ /i/ /k/; 4/ /s/ /w/ /i/ /ng/; 5. /t/ /e/ /n/ /t/.

Name ______________________________

Listen to each word your teacher says. Add the sound. Circle the picture of the new word you made.

1.

 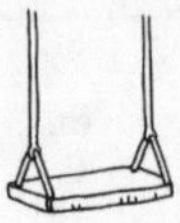 

2.

3.

 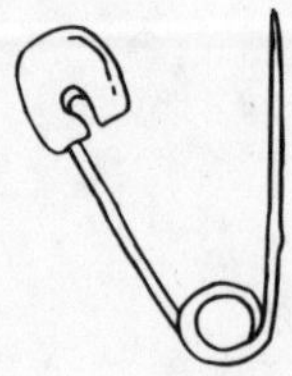 

4.

5.

Teacher Directions: Explain to children that we can add a sound to a word to make a new word. Model item 1 by saying: *win. I can add /g/ to the ending of* win *to make a new word: /wwwiiinnng/,* wing. Guide children to circle the picture of the wing. 2. Say *lamb*. Tell children to add /p/ to the ending of *lamb*. 3. Say *pin*. Tell children to add /k/ to the ending of *pin*. 4. Say *rib*. Tell children to add /k/ to the beginning of *rib*. 5. Say *lock*. Tell children to add /k/ to the beginning of *lock*.

Name ______________________________

The word **at** has a short **a** sound.

Add **e** to the end to make **ate**.

The **a_e** spelling makes the long **a** sound in **ate**.

A. Read the words in the box. Listen for the long a sound. Write the word that names each picture.

gate	tape	snake	grape

1. ______________ 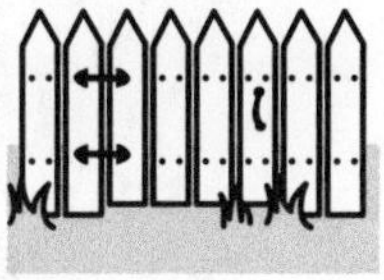

2. ______________ 

3. ______________ 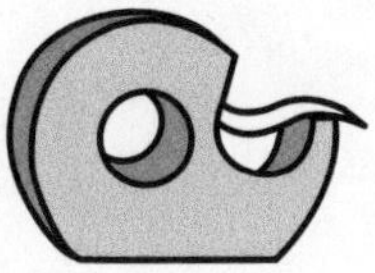

4. ______________ 

B. Write your own sentence using a word from the box.

____

Name ____________________

A. Use the words in the box to complete the sentences.

late	shape	lake	chase	whale	tape

1. Ken is ______________ for school.

2. Tam can use ______________ on the box.

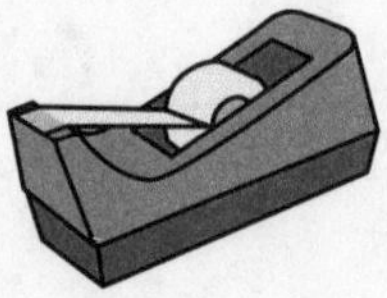

3. A ______________ can swim.

4. What ______________ is this?

B. Add one letter to make a new word with the long <u>a</u> sound. Then write the word.

1. at ______________ **2.** can ______________

Name ______________________________

Fold back the paper along the dotted line. Use the blanks to write each word as it is read aloud. When you finish the test, unfold the paper. Use the list at the right to correct any spelling mistakes.

1. ____________ 1. make
2. ____________ 2. take
3. ____________ 3. came
4. ____________ 4. game
5. ____________ 5. gate
6. ____________ 6. late

High-Frequency Words

7. ____________ 7. some
8. ____________ 8. today

Name ____

A. Read the words in the box. Then sort the words using the word endings.

came	gate	game	take	make	late

Words with <u>ame</u>	Words with <u>ake</u>	Words with <u>ate</u>

B. Think of words that have the same word endings. Add them to the chart.

Name ______________________________

A. Read the words in the box. Then sort the words using the word endings.

came	take	make	game

Words with ame	**Words with ake**

B. Think of words that have the same word endings. Add them to the chart.

Name ______________________________

A. Read the words in the box. Then sort the words.

came gate game make late page take space

Words with <u>ate</u>	Words with <u>ame</u>	Words with <u>ace</u>

Words with <u>ake</u>	Words with <u>age</u>

B. Add new words with the same word endings.

Name ____________________

make	take	came	game	gate
late	chin	graph	some	today

A. Write a spelling word for each clue.

1. You play this with a pal. ____________________

2. This is by your lips. ____________________

3. You make this in math class. ____________________

B. Write a spelling word to complete the sentence.

4. I will ____________________ the bus.

5. I will go to school ____________________.

Name ______________________________

Trace and write D and d. Then copy the sentence. Make sure to leave spaces between words. Write neatly.

D D D D D

D D D

d d d d d d d

d d d

Dan dives deep.

Name ______________________________

A **contraction** is a short form of two words. An **apostrophe** (') takes the place of the missing letters. Read the words: **is not**. Now read the contraction: **isn't**.

The apostrophe (') in **isn't** stands for the letter **o**.

Write the contraction for the two words.

1. was + not = ______________

2. can + not = ______________

3. has + not = ______________

4. are + not = ______________

Name ____

A. Read the contractions in ( ). Circle the word that completes each sentence.

1. Jack the dog (isn't, is'nt) taking a bath.

2. Kate (ca'nt, can't) get him in the tub.

3. Jack still (has'nt, hasn't) taken a bath!

B. Use a contraction you wrote above to complete the sentence.

4. Nate ______________________ go!

C. Use one of the words you circled above to write a new sentence.

____

____

Name ______________________________

A. Read the sentences out loud. Match each sentence to the picture.

1. This is the **way** to camp. **a.** 

2. I see the school **now**. **b.** 

3. I can not go out **today**. **c.** 

4. He can have **some** grapes. **d.** 

5. **Why** is the pup sad? **e.** 

6. I can put this **away**. **f.** 

Name ________________________________

A **verb** is a word that shows action.

Examples: Nate swims.
Mom waves.

Find the verb in each group.
Draw a circle around the verb.

1.	Pam	hat	sit
2.	me	lake	smile
3.	kick	fun	ball
4.	not	hops	Sam
5.	runs	red	pup

Name ____________________

A. Read the draft model. Find the errors.

Draft Model

That duck a lot!

The ducks to the laek.

B. Fix the draft by adding a verb to each sentence. Use the long a spelling pattern to correct any spelling errors.

____

____

____

Connect to Writing

C. Look in your writer's notebook. Check to see if you used verbs correctly. Remember to use the long a spelling pattern for words such as gate.

____

Name ______________________________

When you write three verbs in a list, put a **comma** after the first two verbs.

Examples: I hop, skip, and run.

commas

A. Circle the commas in the sentences.

1. I will mix, bake, and sell this cake!

2. It is fun to run, catch, and pitch in the game.

3. My cat licks, naps, and plays all day.

B. Put commas in the sentences where they belong.

4. Kate runs hops and skips to win the race.

5. My dog sits runs and naps.

6. Jane likes to read bake and sing.

Whale at the Lake

Whale is on skates.

He is going to the lake.

Teacher Directions: Have children establish a purpose for reading the take-home story.

Now, Whale is in.

The pals have fun!

Connect to Community: Have children talk to a family member about activities they like to do with their pals.

Whale can't see his pals.

Where did they go?

"Here we are!" they yell.

They wave to Whale and tell him to come in.

Name ______________________________

Alliteration is when you repeat the beginning sound in two or more words.

Example: Mom made muffins.

Listen to the sentences your teacher says. Circle the picture of the sentence with alliteration.

1.

2.

3.

4.

Teacher Directions: Read the box at the top of the page aloud. Read the sample sentence and emphasize the /m/ sounds at the beginning of each word. Explain that this sentence is an example of alliteration. 1. Say: *Ken can catch.* Then say: *Kate and Pam like to swim.* 2. Say: *We take the bus to school.* Then say: *Chad and Chip are chums.* 3. Say: *The lion roars loudly.* Then say: *Fred finds fresh fruit.* 4. Say: *Beautiful blossoms begin to bloom.* Then say: *The lake and trees are so pretty.*

Name ______________________________

Listen to each word your teacher says. Take away the sound. Circle the picture of the new word you made.

1.

2.

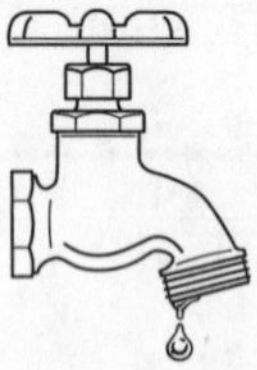

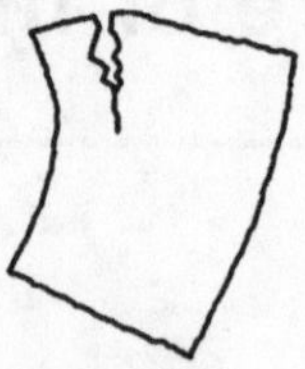

3.

4.

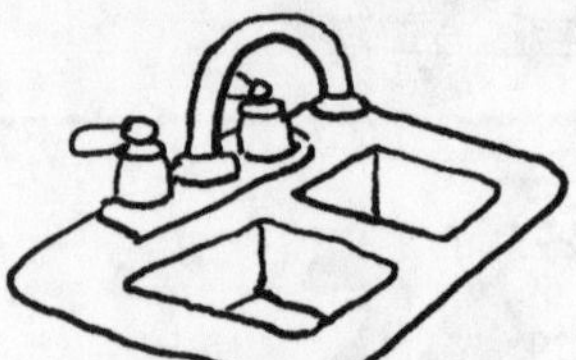

5.

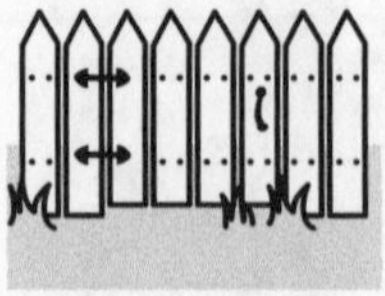

Teacher Directions: Explain to children that we can take away a sound from a word to make a new word. Model item 1 by saying *fang. I can take away /g/ from the ending of fang to make a new word: /fffaaannn/,* fan. Guide children to circle the picture of the fan 2. Say *drip.* Tell children to take away /d/ from the beginning of *drip.* 3. Say *rang.* Tell children to take away /g/ from the ending of *rang.* 4. Say *think.* Tell children to take away /th/ from the beginning of *think.* 5. Say *pride.* Tell children to take away /p/ from the beginning of *pride.*

Name ______________________________

The word **rid** has a short **i** sound.

Add **e** to the end to make **ride**.

The **i_e** spelling stands for the long **i** sound you hear in ride.

A. Read the words in the box. Listen for the long i sound. Write the word that names each picture.

smile	dime	kite	bike

1. ______________ 

2. ______________ 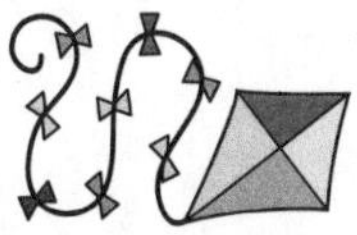

3. ______________ 

4. ______________ 

B. Write your own sentence using a word from above.

____

____

Name ______________________________

A. Read the words. Circle the word that has the long i sound. Write the word on the line.

1. will slide slid ____________

2. nine his nip ____________

3. fin pin fine ____________

4. bit lick bite ____________

5. pine pin dip ____________

B. Add one letter to make a new word with the short i sound. Then write the word.

1. quit ____________ 2. rip ____________

Name ______________________

Fold back the paper along the dotted line. Use the blanks to write each word as it is read aloud. When you finish the test, unfold the paper. Use the list at the right to correct any spelling mistakes.

1. ______________ 1. like
2. ______________ 2. spike
3. ______________ 3. ride
4. ______________ 4. hide
5. ______________ 5. bike
6. ______________ 6. mine

High-Frequency Words

7. ______________ 7. water
8. ______________ 8. should

Name ______________________________

A. Read the words in the box. Then sort the words using the word endings.

bike	hide	like	mine	ride	spike

Words with ide	Words with ike	Words with ine

B. Think of words that have the same word endings. Add them to the chart.

Name ______________________________

A. Read the words in the box. Then sort the words using the word endings.

bike	hide	like	ride

Words with <u>ike</u>	Words with <u>ide</u>
________	________
________	________
________	________
________	________

B. Think of words that have the same word endings. Add them to the chart.

Name ______________________________

A. Read the words in the box. Then sort the words using the word endings.

bike	hide	like	mine	ride	shine	spike	twice

Words with <u>ide</u>	Words with <u>ine</u>	Words with <u>ice</u>	Words with <u>ike</u>

B. Think of words that have the same word endings. Add them to the chart.

Name ______________________________

A. Circle and write the word that is spelled correctly.

like lik

1. ______________________

rid ride

2. ______________________

water watre

3. ______________________

B. Write the word that completes the sentence.

mak make

4. We can help ______________________ lunch.

Name ____________________

Trace and write V and v. Then copy the sentence.
Make sure to leave spaces between words. Write neatly.

Vv

The vet has a van.

Name ________________________________

Add -s to the end of a word to name more than one person or thing. Read the words. Listen for the sounds at the end of **bikes**.

bike  **bikes**

A. Add -s to the word to name more than one thing. Read the sentences.

1. grape ____________________

2. dime ____________________

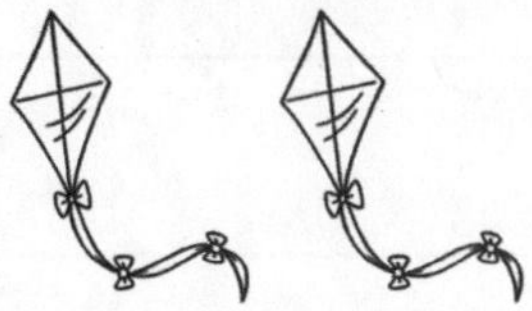

3. kite ____________________

B. Write your own sentence. Use a word that names more than one thing.

____

____

Name ______________________________

A. Circle the word that completes each sentence.

1. Mike and Kate ran two (mile, miles).

2. Then they went for a (hike, hikes).

3. They ate a lot of (graps, grapes).

4. Clive and Shane ride the (biks, bikes).

5. Jane has five (vases, vase) for the plants.

B. Use one of the words you circled above to write a new sentence.

____

____

____

Name ______________________________

Read the words in the box. Complete each sentence. Use one of the words in the box.

green	grow	together	should	pretty	water

1. They walk up the hill ______________.

2. My dog likes the ______________.

3. He will ______________ tall.

4. Where ______________ we go?

5. The pig can eat ______________ grass.

6. The bride is ______________.

Name ______________________________

Present-tense verbs tell about action that happens now. When a present-tense verb tells about one noun, it ends in **-s.**

Example: Jane jumps.

When a present-tense verb tells about more than one noun or the pronoun **I** or **you,** it does not end in **-s.**

Examples: Jane and Ann jump. I jump.

Choose the correct present-tense verb in ( ) to complete each sentence. Write the verb on the line.

1. Sam ____________ to the lake. (hike, hikes)

2. Ken and Sal ____________ a kite. (make, makes)

3. Jen ____________ in the sun. (play, plays)

4. I ____________ it go up. (see, sees)

Name ________________________________

A. Read the draft. Find the errors in present-tense verbs.

Draft Model

Beth and Mike likes bikes.
Mike want to ride my biek.
I lends it to him.

B. Revise the draft by fixing the errors. Make sure you use present-tense verbs correctly. Use the long i spelling pattern to correct any spelling errors.

Connect to Writing

C. Look in your writer's notebook. Check that you used present-tense verbs correctly. Remember to use the long i spelling pattern for words such as kite.

Name ______________________________

The important words in a **play title** begin with a capital letter.

The first word of a play title is always capitalized.

The title of a play is underlined.

Example:
The Three Bears
is a fun play.

Underline the play title that is correct.

1. Two Mice Run
   two mice run

2. We play the Drum
   We Play the Drum

3. Frog Can Hop
   Frog can hop

4. we Help dad
   We Help Dad

Mom: I like plants.

You made me smile!

Kate: We are glad!

Mike: Get well, Mom!

Connect to Community: Have children talk to a family member about a gift they gave someone.

A Gift for Mom

Mike: Mom is sick.

Kate: Let's get a gift.

Teacher Directions: Have children establish a purpose for reading the take-home story.

Mike: I can shop.
Kate: Let's go together.

(2)

Mike: Look! Plants!
Kate: Mom likes plants.

(3)

Name ______________________________

Words that rhyme end with the same sounds.

Say each picture name. Then draw a picture of something whose name rhymes with it.

1. 	
2. 	
3. 	
4. 	
5. 	

Teacher Directions: Read the box at the top of the page aloud. Point to the pictures as you say the words: *bed, head, bread.* Point out that these words rhyme.

Name ______________________________

Say the name of each picture. Count the sounds in each word. Then draw an X in one box for each sound.

1. 				
2. 				
3. 				
4. 				
5. 				

Teacher Directions: Model item 1 by saying *mane.* Say: *I can say the sounds in the word* mane. *The word mane has three sounds: /m/ /ā/ /n/. Say the sounds with me: /m/ /ā/ /n/.*

Name ______________________________

Sometimes the letter c makes the **s** sound. You can hear it in **race** and **nice**.

The letter **g** can make the **j** sound. You hear it in **wage** and **gel**.

The letters **dge** together also make the **j** sound, as in **badge** and **ledge**.

Say the word. Write the word. Circle the picture that shows the word.

1. trace ______________________________

2. stage ______________________________

3. lodge ______________________________

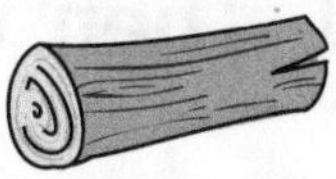

4. bridge ______________________________

Name ____________________

A. Read the words in the box. Write the words that complete the sentences.

hedge	cage	edge

I. Pip the pet sits in a ____________ .

2. Mom cuts the top ____________ of the can.

3. Pam trims the ____________ .

B. Change one letter to make a new word with the soft c or g sound. Then write the word.

I. late ____________ 2. hem ____________

Name ____________________

Fold back the paper along the dotted line. Use the blanks to write each word as it is read aloud. When you finish the test, unfold the paper. Use the list at the right to correct any spelling mistakes.

1. ____________ **1. rice**

2. ____________ **2. nice**

3. ____________ **3. page**

4. ____________ **4. age**

5. ____________ **5. wedge**

6. ____________ **6. ledge**

High-Frequency Words

7. ____________ **7. from**

8. ____________ **8. once**

Name ______________________________

A. Read the words in the box. Then sort the words using the word endings.

age ledge nice page rice wedge

Words with ge	Words with ce	Words with dge

B. Think of words that have the same word endings. Add them to the chart.

Name ______________________________

A. Read the words in the box. Then sort the words using the word endings.

age	rice	edge	ice

Words with ge	Words with ce	Words with dge

B. Think of words that have the same word endings. Add them to the chart.

Name ______________________________

A. Read the words in the box. Then sort the words.

hedge	nice	ledge	page	price	wage	rice	wedge

Words with <u>ge</u>	Words with <u>ce</u>	Words with <u>dge</u>

B. Add new words to the chart with the same endings.

Name ______________________________

Read each word in the box. Say each word.

rice	nice	page	age
wedge	ledge	from	once

Use the clues to write a spelling word on the line.

1. starts like **leg** + ends like **hedge** ______________

2. starts like **nine** + ends like **price** ______________

3. starts like **pale** + ends like **cage** ______________

4. starts like **web** + ends like **pledge** ______________

5. starts like **frame** + ends like **Tom** ______________

Name ______________________________

Trace and write Y and y. Then copy the sentence. Make sure to leave spaces between words. Write neatly.

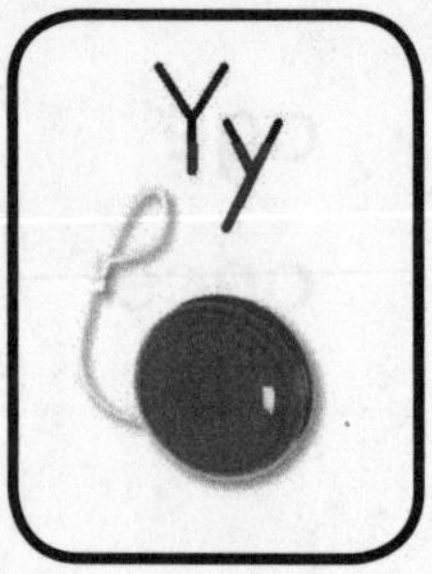

Yoko has a yoyo.

Name ____________________

Add -**ed** to an action word to tell what happened in the past. Add -**ing** to an action word to tell what is happening now.

Look at the word **race**. It ends with the letter e.
To add -**ed** or -**ing**, first drop the e.

race - e + ed = raced   **race - e + ing = racing**

A. Add -ing to each word. Write the new word.

I. trace ____________________

2. skate ____________________

B. Add -ed to each word. Write the new word.

3. rake ____________________

4. slice ____________________

Name ______________________________

A. Read each sentence. Add -ing or -ed to the word in ( ). Read the word. Complete each sentence.

1. Dave ____________________ to the park. (race)

2. Dad is ____________________ to us. (wave)

B. Read the words in ( ). Circle the word that completes each sentence.

3. Mike is (danced, dancing) to a song.

4. He (baked, baking) a cake.

5. Pam is (sliced, slicing) the bread.

C. Use a word you circled above to write a new sentence.

____

____

Name ______________________________

A. Read the sentences out loud. Match each sentence to the picture.

1. Cal is **happy** in the tent.

2. **Once** I jumped on a box.

3. I was **so** fast, I won the race.

4. The fish came **from** the pond.

5. We can play **any** game.

6. The boy wished **upon** a star.

a.

b.

c.

d.

e.

f.

Name ______________________________

Past-tense verbs tell about action that happened in the past. Most verbs in the past tense end in **-ed**.

Example: Dave fixed the gate yesterday.

Future-tense verbs tell about action that is going to happen. Add **will** before a verb to form the future tense.

Example: Dave will fix the gate on Friday.

A. Read the sentences. Write the past tense of the verb in ( ) to complete each sentence.

1. Dad ______________ Spot in a tub. (wash)

2. Jed ______________ up the hose. (pick)

B. Write the future tense of the verb in ( ).

1. Sam ______________ the bus. (ride)

2. Chuck ______________ with Bob. (skate)

Name ______________________________

A. Read the draft. Find the errors in past- and future-tense verbs.

Draft Model

Jake will rakeed the leaves yesterday.
He gazeed at the clouds tomorrow.

B. Revise the draft by fixing the errors. Use past- and future-tense verbs correctly. Remember the spelling rule to drop the e when adding -ed or -ing to words that end with e.

____

____

Connect to Writing

C. Look in your writer's notebook. Make sure you used past- and future-tense verbs correctly. Remember the spelling rule to drop the e when adding -ed or -ing to words that end with e.

Name ____

When you write three or more words in a list, put a **comma** after the first two words.

Example: I ate ham, bread, and eggs.

commas

A. Circle the commas in the sentence.

1. We like cats, dogs, and fish.

B. Add commas to the sentences.

2. We will dress up in wigs hats and capes.

3. I will wash my red pink and white pack.

4. The frog jumped over the stick bug and rake.

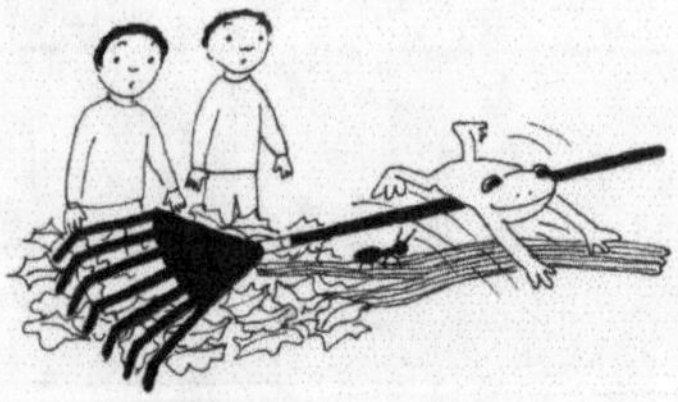

5. Kent will see Gen Pam and June at school.

Little Buck helped Fred.

They got to Gran's.

They had fudge!

Connect to Community: Have children talk to a family member about a food they like to eat with friends and family.

4

Little Fred and Little Buck

Gran liked fudge.

Mom was making some.

Fred walked to Gran's with it.

Teacher Directions: Have children establish a purpose for reading the take-home story.

1

There are too many trees.
Where is the path? Little
Fred is lost!

②

Little Buck came by.
"Can you help me?"
asked Fred.

③

Name ____

**Say the name of each picture. Count the sounds.
Draw an X in one box for each sound.**

1. 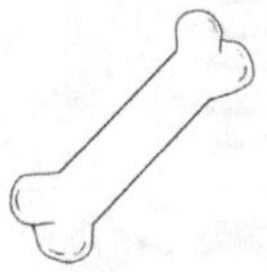				
2. 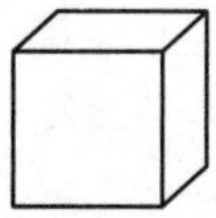				
3. 				
4. 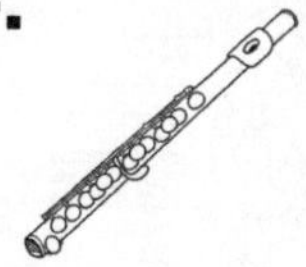				
5. 				

Teacher Directions: Model item 1 by saying *bone.* Say: *I can say the sounds in the word* bone. *The word* bone *has three sounds: /b/ /ō/ /n/. Say the sounds with me: /b/ /ō/ /n/.*

Name ______________________________

Say each picture name. Circle the picture whose name has the same middle sound as the first picture in the row.

1.   

2.   

3.   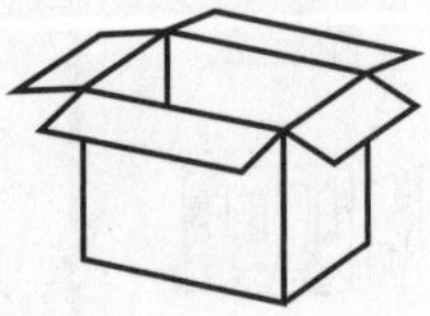

4.  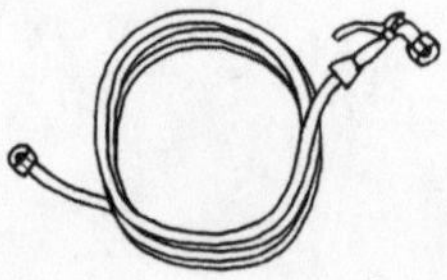 

5. 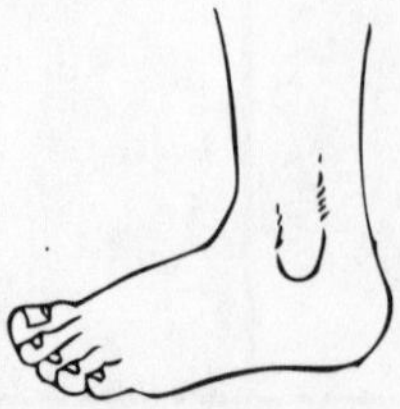  

Teacher Directions: Model item 1 by saying /m/ /ī/ /s/. Emphasize the vowel sound. Then say *face* and *hive* and explicitly compare vowel sounds. Say: *The words* mice *and* hive *have the same middle sound: /ī/.* Face *has a different middle sound*: /ā/. Guide children to circle the picture of the hive.

Name ____

The letters **o_e** stand for the long **o** sound.
The long **o** sound is the middle sound in **rope**.

The letters **u_e** stand for the long **u** sound.
The long **u** sound is the first sound in **use**.

The letters **e_e** stand for the long **e** sound.
The long **e** sound is the middle sound in **Pete**.

A. Circle and write the word that names the picture.

1. 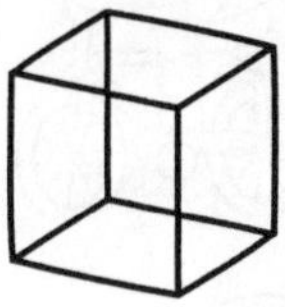

cub cube

2. 

note not

3. 

mull mule

4. 

glob globe

B. Write o, u, or e to complete each word.

5. 

r ________ se

6. 

c ________ ne

Name ______________________________

A. Use the words in the box to complete each sentence. Write the word on the line.

huge	stove	Eve	these	rode	cone

I. Its trunk is ______________________!

2. Pete ______________________ on his bike.

3. My name is ______________________.

4. Do you like ______________________ pants?

B. Add one letter to make a new word with a long vowel sound. Then write the word.

I. hop ______________________ 2. not ______________________

Name ______________________________

Fold back the paper along the dotted line. Use the blanks to write each word as it is read aloud. When you finish the test, unfold the paper. Use the list at the right to correct any spelling mistakes.

1. ____________ **1. hope**

2. ____________ **2. nose**

3. ____________ **3. note**

4. ____________ **4. rope**

5. ____________ **5. cute**

6. ____________ **6. cube**

High-Frequency Words

7. ____________ **7. ago**

8. ____________ **8. people**

Name ____________________

A. Read the words in the box. Then sort the words.

cube	cute	nose	note	hope	rope

Words with <u>ute</u>	Words with <u>ose</u>	Words with <u>ube</u>
Words with <u>ope</u>	**Words with <u>ote</u>**	

B. Add words to the chart that have the same endings.

Name ______________________________

A. Read the words in the box. Then sort the words.

cube cute nose note

Words with <u>ute</u>	Words with <u>ose</u>
______ ______ ______	______ ______ ______
Words with <u>ube</u>	**Words with <u>ote</u>**
______ ______ ______	______ ______ ______

B. Add words to the chart that have the same endings.

Name ______________________________

A. Read the words in the box. Then sort the words.

close cube cute hope nose note quote rope

Words with ute	Words with ose	Words with ube
Words with ope	**Words with ote**	

B. Add words to the chart with the same endings.

Name ____________________

Pick the word that is spelled correctly. Write the word to complete the sentence.

1. The ____________ are glad.

   people   peeple

2. I ____________ you will get a bike!

   hoope   hope

3. The cat is ____________ .

   neic   nice

4. The chick is ____________ .

   cuet   cute

5. Use ____________ to tie things.

   rope   ropp

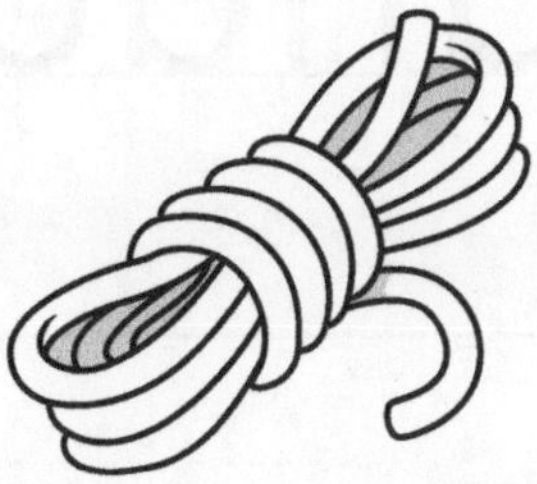

Name ________________________________

Trace and write W and w. Then copy the sentence. Make sure to leave spaces between words. Write neatly.

Ww

W W W W W

W W W

w w w w w w w w w

w w w

Wanda will win.

Name ______________________________

The spellings **a_e, i_e, o_e, u_e,** and **e_e** stay together in the same syllable. The syllable usually has a long vowel sound.

in/<u>side</u> **a/<u>wake</u>** **<u>rose</u>/bud**

Read each word. Draw a line to divide the word into syllables. Write one syllable on each line. Then circle the syllable with the long vowel sound.

1. explode ______________ ______________

2. handshake ______________ ______________

3. sunshine ______________ ______________

4. placemat ______________ ______________

Name ______________________________

A. Read each word. Draw a line to divide the word into syllables. Then circle the syllable with the long vowel sound.

1. flagpole

2. complete

3. costume

B. Use one of the words above to write a new sentence.

Name ______________________________

A. Use the words from the box to complete each sentence. Circle the picture that matches the sentence.

ago	boy	girl	how	old	people

1. This ____________ has a cap.

2. Some ____________ live here.

3. We rode in carts long ____________ .

4. This plate is very ____________ .

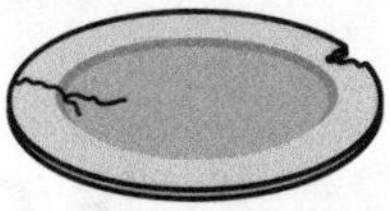

5. This ____________ is in school.

6. This is ____________ to fish.

Name ______________________________

The verbs <u>is</u> and <u>are</u> tell about action happening now.
Use the verb <u>is</u> to tell about one person, place, or thing.

Example: Chad <u>is</u> home.

Use the verb <u>are</u> to tell about more than one person, place, or thing.

Example: Mom and Dad <u>are</u> home.

Circle the verb in each sentence.
Write <u>1</u> if the verb tells about one.
Write <u>2</u> if the verb tells about more than one.

1. The Sun is up. ________

2. Kate and Sam are at school. ________

3. The cat is on the step. ________

4. This game is fun. ________

Name ______________________________

A. Read the draft model. Find the errors.

Draft Model

Seth and Jan is playing.
They is in the water.
Gabe doev in the water, too!

B. Revise the draft by fixing the errors you found. Make sure you use the words is and are correctly. Use the long o spelling pattern to correct any spelling errors.

____

____

____

____

Connect to Writing

C. Look in your writer's notebook. Check to see if you used the words is and are correctly. Remember to use the long o spelling pattern for words such as rope.

Name ______________________________

Use **commas** in a date

- between the day and the month and
- between the date number and the year.

Example: Today is Monday, May 8, 2017.

A. Underline the sentences with the date written correctly.

1. I will see Gran on Friday, June 16, 2017.

   I will see Gran on Friday June 16, 2017.

2. School is out on Tuesday, May 9, 2017.

   School is out on Tuesday, May 9 2017.

3. Today is Monday August 14, 2017.

   Today is Monday, August 14, 2017.

B. Add commas to fix the sentence.

4. We can go on Friday July 7 2017.

Boys and girls still had time to play. They had fun just as you do!

Connect to Community: Have children talk to a family member about ways they help at home.

4

Life Long Ago

What was life like long ago?

What did boys and girls do?

They helped a lot at home.

Teacher Directions: Have children establish a purpose for reading the take-home story.

1

Boys and girls helped
make things.

They helped plant.

②

Boys and girls fed the hens.

They looked for eggs.

③

Name ______________________________

Say the name of each picture. Count the sounds in each word. Then draw an X in one box for each sound.

1. 				
2. 				
3. 				
4. 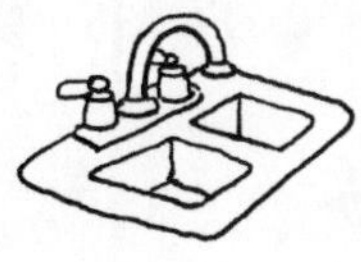				
5. 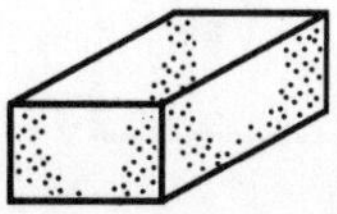				

Teacher Directions: Model item I by saying *book*. Say: *I can say the sounds in the word* book. *The word* book *has three sounds: /b/ /ů/ /k/. Say the sounds with me: /b/ /ů/ /k/.* Guide children to draw three X's for item I.

Name ____

Listen to the sounds your teacher says. Blend the sounds together. Draw a picture of the word you made.

1.	**2.**
3.	**4.**

Teacher Directions: Model item 1 by saying */e/ /g/. Listen as I blend these sounds together: /eeeg/, egg.* Model drawing an egg in the first box and have children copy. For items 2-4, have children listen to the sounds and blend them to form a word. **2. Say:** /m/ /i/ /n/ /t/; **3. Say:** /l/ /u/ /n/ /ch/; **4. Say:** /b/ /ů/ /k/.

Name ______________________________

The letters oo and u can make the middle sound you hear in **book**.

Circle the word in each row that has the same middle sound you hear in took. Write the word.

1. shake	shook	stop	______________
2. hook	rope	nut	______________
3. foot	tune	fudge	______________
4. fun	flop	full	______________
5. rush	patch	push	______________

Name ______________________________

A. Read the words in the box. Listen for the middle sound spelled oo or u. Then write each word next to a word with the same ending sounds.

foot	pull	cook	push

1. book ______________ 2. soot ______________

3. bush ______________ 4. full ______________

B. Change one letter to make a new word with the middle sound you hear in book. Then write the word.

1. bill ______________ 2. pat ______________

Name ______________________________

Fold back the paper along the dotted line. Use the blanks to write each word as it is read aloud. When you finish the test, unfold the paper. Use the list at the right to correct any spelling mistakes.

1. ______________ **1. book**

2. ______________ **2. look**

3. ______________ **3. cook**

4. ______________ **4. took**

5. ______________ **5. hood**

6. ______________ **6. wood**

High-Frequency Words

7. ______________ **7. buy**

8. ______________ **8. done**

Name ____________________

A. Read the words in the box. Then sort the words using the word endings.

book	cook	hood	look	took	wood

Words with <u>ood</u>	**Words with <u>ook</u>**
______	______
______	______
______	______
______	______
______	______
______	______

B. Think of words that have the same word endings. Add them to the chart.

Name ______________________________

A. Read the words in the box. Then sort the words using the word endings.

book	hood	look	took

Words with <u>ood</u>	**Words with <u>ook</u>**

B. Think of words that have the same word endings. Add them to the chart.

Name ______________________________

A. Read the words in the box. Then sort the words.

book hood booklet cook wood look cookie took

Words with ood	**Words with ook**

B. Add words to the chart with the same spellings.

Name ______________________________

book	look	cook	took	hood
wood	nose	cute	buy	done

Is the underlined word spelled correctly? Fill in the circle Yes or No. If the word is spelled wrong, write the word correctly.

1. Lok at all the hens! ____________

   Correct? ○ Yes ○ No

2. Dad will cook eggs at home. ____________

   Correct? ○ Yes ○ No

3. When will they be donne? ____________

   Correct? ○ Yes ○ No

4. The little chicks are cuet. ____________

   Correct? ○ Yes ○ No

Name ________________________________

Trace and write <u>B</u> and <u>b</u>. Then copy the sentence. Make sure to leave spaces between words. Write neatly.

Bb

B B B B B B

B B B

b b b b b b b b b

b b b

Beth has a blue bat.

Name ______________________________

When you add -**ed** or -**ing** to the end of a word that ends with a vowel and a consonant, double the last consonant.

drop + ed = drop + **p** + **ed** = drop**ped**

drop + ing = drop + **p** + **ing** = drop**ping**

A. Add -ed to each word. Write the new word.

1. grab ______________ **2.** slam ______________

3. tag ______________ **4.** stop ______________

B. Add -ing to each word. Write the new word.

5. hug ______________ **6.** plan ______________

7. drip ______________ **8.** skip ______________

Name ______________________________

A. Read the words in ( ). Circle the word that completes each sentence. Then read the sentence out loud.

1. Pam (stopped, stoped) at the store.

2. Brad is (skipped, skipping).

3. Dad (hugged, hugging) my dog Skip.

4. I (grabed, grabbed) an apple from the table.

5. Mom (stopped, stoped) at the red light.

B. Use one of the words you circled above to write a new sentence.

____

____

Name ______________________________

A. Read and spell each word in the box. Complete each sentence. Use one of the words in the box.

done	soon	every	after	work	buy

1. They will go to the park ____________ school.

2. He has a lot of ____________ to do.

3. Matt will ____________ a hat.

4. Now she is ____________!

5. There are dots on ____________ sock.

6. He will wake the cat ____________.

Name ________________________________

A **contraction** is a short way of writing two words. Two words are put together and some letters are left out.

An apostrophe (') takes the place of the o in contractions formed with **not**.

Example: He **isn't** here. (is not = isn't)

Look at the underlined contraction.
Circle the two words used to make the contraction.

1. Jon wasn't at school today.

   Jon was not at school today.

2. Jon doesn't like to stay home.

   Jon does not like to stay home.

3. Mom isn't letting him play with Pal.

   Mom is not letting him play with Pal.

4. He can't ride his bike.

   He can not ride his bike.

Name ______________________________

A. Read the draft model. Find the errors.

Draft Model

The plant stoped growing.
It can'not get sun here.

B. Revise the draft by fixing the errors. Make sure you use contractions correctly. Remember the spelling rule to double the last consonant when adding -ed or -ing to words that end with a vowel and a consonant.

____

____

____

____

Connect to Writing

C. Look in your writer's notebook. Check that you used contractions correctly. Remember the spelling rule to double the last consonant when adding -ed or -ing when necessary.

Name ______________________________

A **contraction** is a short way of writing two words.

Use an **apostrophe** (’) to take the place of the missing letter <u>o</u>.

Circle the contractions that are not correct.
Write the contractions correctly.
Write C if the contraction is correct.

1. This plant isnt’ growing. ______________

2. It ca’nt get sun here. ______________

3. The plant doesnt like this place. ______________

4. It can’t grow and get big at all. ______________

5. The plant is glad it is’nt in the shade now. ______________

Then we buy beans.
We cook the food.
Yum! It is good!

Connect to Community: Have children talk to a family member about their favorite foods.

The Food We Eat

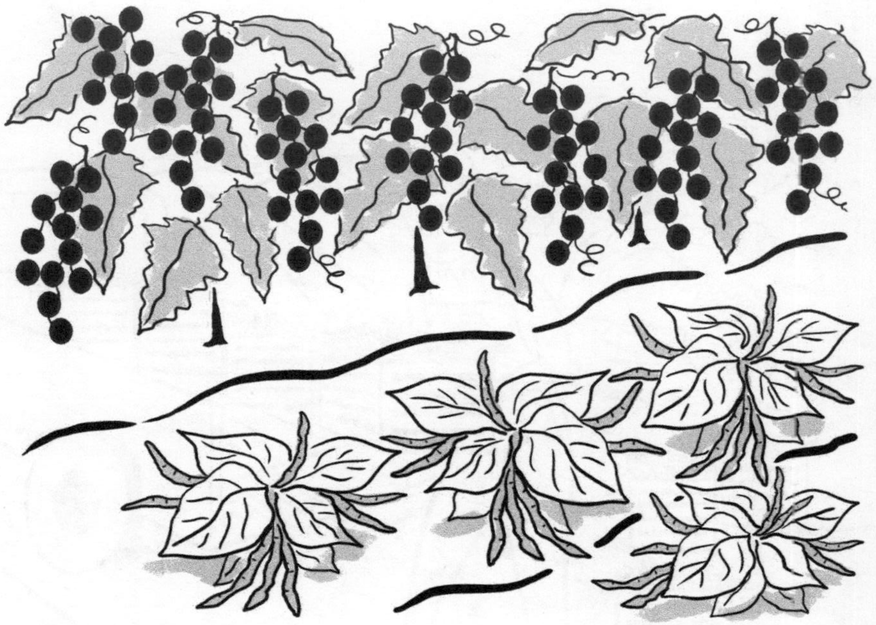

This is a big crop.
It grows beans and grapes.
Soon they can be picked.

Teacher Directions: Have children establish a purpose for reading the take-home story.

People work here. They pack up the food. Then trucks take it to shops.

After that, we go to a shop. We buy the grapes. They look good!

Name ______________________________

Words that rhyme end with the same sounds.

drip 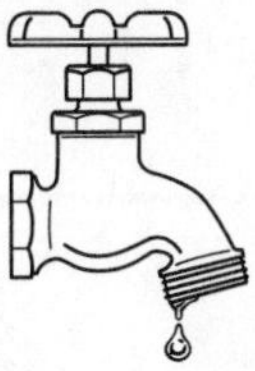 **rip** 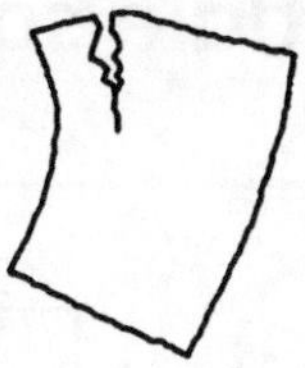 **lip** 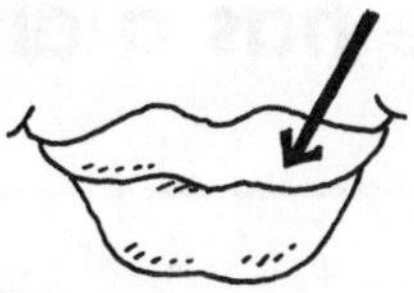

Say each picture name. Then draw two pictures of things whose names rhymes with it.

1. 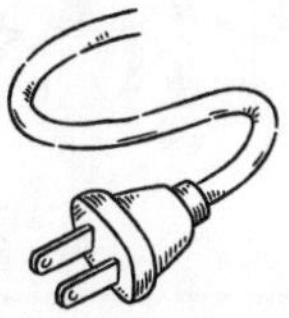		
2. 		
3. 		
4. 		
5. 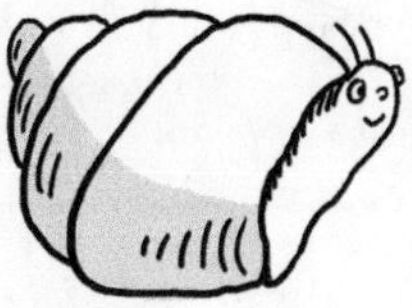		

Teacher Directions: Read the box at the top of the page, and point to the pictures as you say each word: *drip, rip, lip.* Point out to children that these words rhyme.

Name ______________________________

Look at each picture. Say the name of each picture out loud. Say the middle sounds. Circle the picture whose name has a different middle sound.

1.

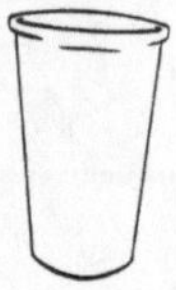 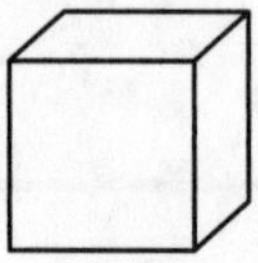 

2.

 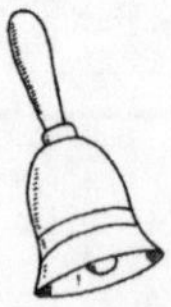 

3.

4.

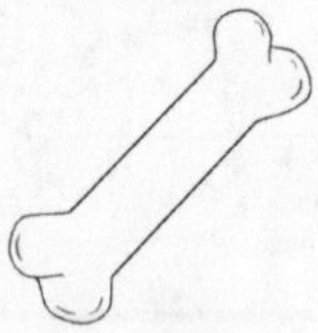  

5.

Teacher Directions: Model item 1 by saying *cup, cube,* and *bug.* Repeat, stressing the difference between the long and short vowel sounds: /u/ and /ū/. Say: *The words* cup *and* bug *have the same middle sound: /u/.* Cube *has a different middle sound: /ū/.* Guide children to circle the picture of the cube.

Name ______________________________

The letters **a**, **ai** and **ay** can make the long **a** sound.

April 

train 
hay 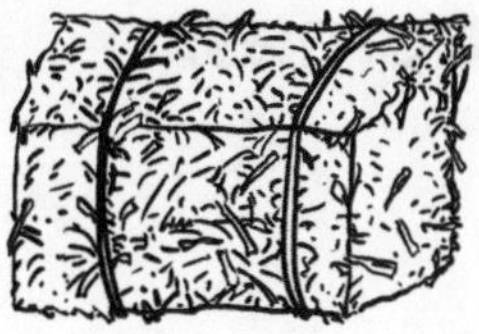

A. Read the words in the box. Write the word that names the picture.

tray	snail	pail	day

1. ______________ 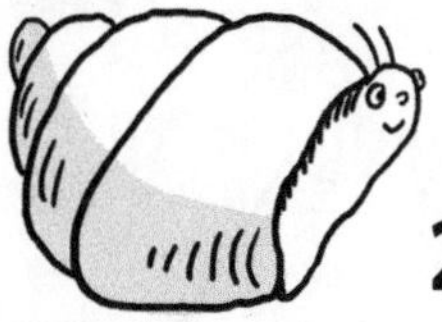

2. ______________ 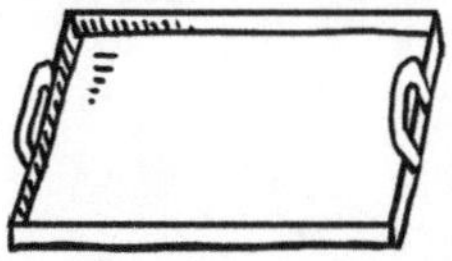

3. ______________ 

4. ______________ 

B. Write your own sentence using a word from the box.

____

Name ______________________________

A. Read each word. Underline the letters that make the long <u>a</u> sound. Write the word. Circle the picture that it names.

1. paint ____________________

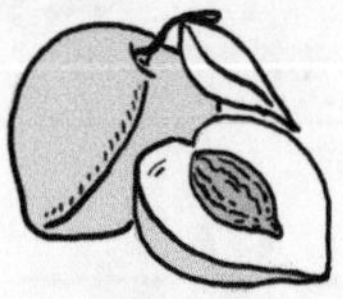

2. clay ____________________

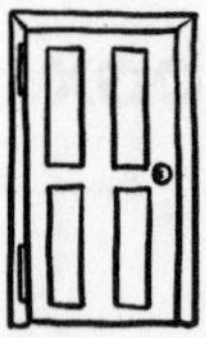

3. train ____________________

4. apron ____________________

B. Add one letter to make a new word with the long <u>a</u> sound. Then write the word.

1. man ____________________ 2. bat ____________________

Name ______________________________

Fold back the paper along the dotted line. Use the blanks to write each word as it is read aloud. When you finish the test, unfold the paper. Use the list at the right to correct any spelling mistakes.

1. ______________ 1. mail

2. ______________ 2. chain

3. ______________ 3. play

4. ______________ 4. rain

5. ______________ 5. way

6. ______________ 6. day

High-Frequency Words

7. ______________ 7. our

8. ______________ 8. carry

Name ____________________

A. Read the words in the box. Then sort the words.

chain	day	mail	play	rain	way

Words with ai	**Words with ay**
____________	____________
____________	____________
____________	____________
____________	____________
____________	____________
____________	____________
____________	____________

B. Add new words with the same spellings to the chart.

Name ____________________

A. Read the words in the box. Then sort the words.

day	mail	main	pay	rain	way

Words with <u>ay</u>	**Words with <u>ai</u>**

B. Think of words that have the same word spellings. Add them to the chart.

Name ______________________________

A. Read the words in the box. Then sort the words.

chain	day	gray	mail
play	rain	snail	way

Words with <u>ai</u>	Words with <u>ay</u>
______	______
______	______
______	______
______	______
______	______
______	______

B. Add new words with the same spellings to the chart.

Name ______________________________

mail	chain	play	rain	way
day	took	hood	our	carry

Read the words in the box. Write the word that completes the sentence.

1. A note came in the ____________.

2. He can ____________ the little log.

3. I pull my ____________ over my head.

4. It will ____________ today.

5. The two whales ____________ in the water.

Name ____________________

Trace and write N and n. Then copy the sentence. Make sure to leave spaces between words. Write neatly.

Nn

N N N N N N

N N N

n n n n n n n n

n n n

Nat naps in the nest.

Name ____________________

A B C D E F G H I J K L M N O P Q R S T U V W X Y Z

We put words in ABC order by looking at the first letter of each word.

If words begin with the same letter, we look at the second letter.

b<u>a</u>t   b<u>e</u>d   b<u>o</u>x

Read the two words. Circle the word in ( ) that comes next in ABC order. Write the word.

1. lap   lead   (log   lash) ____________

2. make   mix   (much   men) ____________

3. sick   slim   (sand   stay) ____________

4. gem   gold   (glad   grip) ____________

Name ______________________________

A. Read the two words. Circle the word in ( ) that comes next in ABC order. Write the word.

1. hail hem (hive hat) ____________

2. cat cone (cent cube) ____________

3. ramp rent (rail rock) ____________

B. Use one of the words you circled above to write a sentence.

____

____

____

Name ______________________________

Complete each sentence. Use one of the words in the box.

about	animal	carry	eight	give	our

1. I will ____________ you this snack.

2. I can use this to ____________ grapes.

3. My dog is ____________ this big.

4. I see ____________ eggs in the nest.

5. This is ____________ home.

6. A pig is an ____________ .

Name ______________________________

special: Something <u>**special**</u> is important or unique.

splendid: Something that is <u>**splendid**</u> is wonderful or very good.

A. Match each sentence to the picture that it tells about.

1. Today is my **special** day.

a. 

2. We had a **splendid** time on our school trip.

b. 

B. Use the words in the box to complete each sentence.

special	splendid

3. The doll is ______________ to me.

4. Mom looks ______________ in her new dress.

Name ______________________________

A **dictionary** is a book that gives the meanings of words. It shows how to use a word in a sentence.

We use a **dictionary** to find out what a word means.

A. Look up the words special and splendid in a dictionary. Write what each word means.

1. special ______________________________

2. splendid ______________________________

B. Use special or splendid to complete each sentence.

3. The school play was ______________.

4. The gift from Mom is ______________ to me.

5. We had a ______________ time with Gram.

Name ____

A **subject** and **verb** must agree. The verbs **was** and **were** tell about the past. **Was** tells about one subject, which can be a person, place, or thing. **Were** tells about more than one subject.

Examples: Fox was at home.
Hen and Duck were on the grass.

Circle the verb that belongs in the sentence.

1. The Sun (was, were) up.
2. Hen and Duck (was, were) playing.
3. Fox (was, were) cooking lunch.
4. Hen (was, were) hungry.
5. He (was, were) waving to them.
6. They (was, were) going to eat lunch with Fox.

Name ______________________________

A. Read the draft model. Find the errors.

Draft Model

Nate was in a play todai.

Josh and Pam was in the play, too.

The play were abuot animales.

B. Fix the errors you found. Make sure the subject and verbs agree. Make sure to spell words with long <u>a</u> correctly.

____

____

____

____

Connect to Writing

C. Look in your writer's notebook. Make sure you used the words <u>was</u> and <u>were</u> correctly and subject and verbs agree.

Name ______________________________

A **contraction** is a short way of saying and writing two words.

An apostrophe (’) takes the place of letters that are left out.

was not ⟶ wasn’t

he is ⟶ he’s

let us ⟶ let’s

Write the contraction for the underlined words in each sentence.

1. Sam and Tate were not at school. ______________

2. We are not running in the rain. ______________

3. He is at home. ______________ .

4. Let us play with the blocks. ______________

A Fox Tail

Fox wanted to eat.
"I see Hen," Fox said. "I will
get an egg from her!"

Teacher Directions: Have children establish a purpose for reading the take-home story.

He asked Hen for an egg.
"Ha!" said Hen. "You can not
trick me. I see a fox tail!"
Hen did not give Fox any eggs.

Connect to Community: Have children talk to a family member about other stories they've read that have trickster characters.

"May I take that egg?"
Fox asked.
"No, you may not!" said Hen.

2

"I will trick Hen and get that egg," said Fox. Fox dressed up. He put on a hat and old pants. He went to see Hen.

3

Name ______________________________

Listen to the sounds your teacher says. Blend the sounds together. Circle the picture that goes with the word you made.

1.

2.

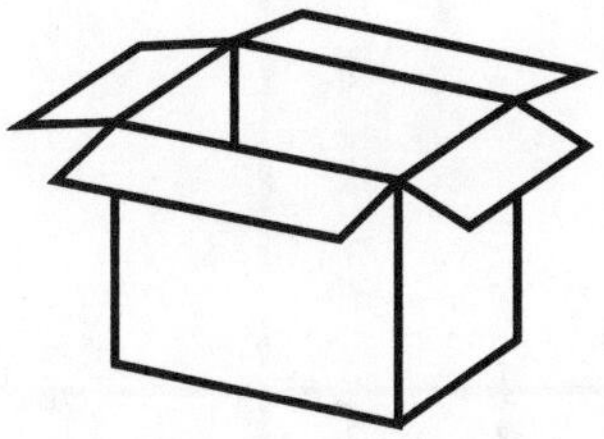

3.

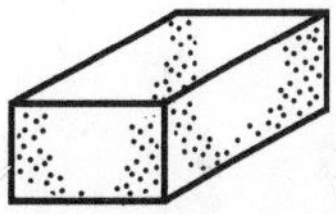

4.

5.

Teacher Directions: Model item I by saying /f/ /o/ /ks/. *I will blend the sounds to make a word: /fffoooksss/, fox.* Guide children to circle the picture of the fox for item I. For items 2–5, say the following sounds. Have students blend the sounds to say each word. Then have them circle the picture that shows it. 2. /b/ /ŭ/ /k/; 3. /b/ /r/ /e/ /d/; 4/ /sh/ /ē/ /p/; 5. /t/ /r/ /ē/.

Name ____

Say the name of each picture. Count the sounds in each word. Then draw an X in one box for each sound.

1. 					
2. 					
3. 					
4. 					
5. 					

Teacher Directions: I. Model: *I can say the sounds in the word* skunk. *The word* skunk *has five sounds: /s/ /k/ /u/ /n/ /k/. Say the sounds with me: /s/ /k/ /u/ /n/ /k/.*

Name ____________________

The long **e** sound can be spelled with the letters **e** as in **be, ee** as in **keep, ea** as in **eat,** and **ie** as in **thief**.

Read the words in the box. Write the words from the box that have the same vowel sound and spelling.

she	sleep	each	deep	shield	seat	me	chief

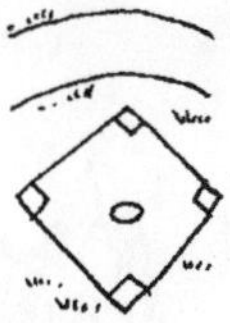

1. field ____________ ____________

2. eat ____________ ____________

3. cheese ____________ ____________

4. he ____________ ____________

Name ______________________________

A. Read the word. Draw a line under the letters that make the long e sound. Write the letters on the line. Circle the matching picture.

1. sheet ____________  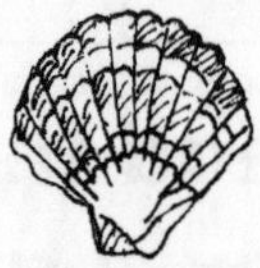

2. team ____________  

3. tree ____________  

4. shield ____________  

B. Add one letter to make a new word with the long e sound. Then write the word.

1. red ____________ 2. step ____________

Name ________________________________

Fold back the paper along the dotted line. Use the blanks to write each word as it is read aloud. When you finish the test, unfold the paper. Use the list at the right to correct any spelling mistakes.

1. ____________ 1. me
2. ____________ 2. feed
3. ____________ 3. seat
4. ____________ 4. we
5. ____________ 5. keep
6. ____________ 6. beak

High-Frequency Words

7. ____________ 7. other

8. ____________ 8. because

Name ______________________________

A. Read the words in the box. Then sort the words.

beak	feed	keep	me	seat	we

Words with ee	Words with e	Words with ea

B. Think of words that have the same spellings. Add them to the chart.

Name ______________________________

A. Read the words in the box. Then sort the words.

eat	feet	keep	me	sea	we

Words with <u>ee</u>	Words with <u>e</u>	Words with <u>ea</u>

B. Think of words that have the same spellings. Add them to the chart.

Name ______________________________

A. Read the words in the box. Then sort the words.

beak feed keep me seat she speed we

Words with <u>ee</u>	Words with <u>e</u>	Words with <u>ea</u>

B. Add new words with the same spellings to the chart.

Name ______________________________

Circle the word that is spelled correctly. Then write the word.

feed fead

1. ______________________

beak beek

2. ______________________

chese cheese

3. ______________________

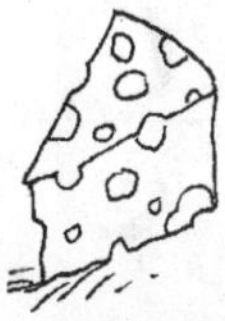

rain rayn

4. ______________________

snale snail

5. ______________________

Name ____________________

Trace and write G and g. Then copy the sentence. Make sure to leave spaces between words. Write neatly.

G G G G G G

G G G

g g g g g g g g g

g g g

Gail gave me grapes.

Name ______________________________

A **prefix** is a word part you can add to the beginning of a word to change its meaning.

The prefix **re-** means **again.**
The prefix **pre-** means **before.**

The prefix **un-** means **not** or **the opposite of.**

redo **precook** **unsafe**

A. Match each sentence to a word with a prefix.

1. She is not happy. — a. unhappy
2. Pat will read the book again. — b. premade
3. The room is not clean. — c. reread
4. I will use the bag again. — d. unclean
5. I made the crust before I baked it. — e. reuse

B. Write a sentence using a word with a prefix.

____

Name ______________________________

A. Write a new word with a prefix to match the words.

1. cook before ______________________

2. heat again ______________________

3. not freeze ______________________

B. Use one of the words you wrote above to write a new sentence.

Name ______________________________

A. Read and spell each word in the box. Use the words in the box to complete each sentence.

into	blue	or	small	other	because

1. Do you want this one ______________ that one?

2. I put on a hat ______________ it is cold.

3. The animal is very ______________ .

4. We walk ______________ the school.

5. The flag is red, white, and ______________ .

6. I will eat the ______________ apple.

Name ____________________

A. Read each clue. Look at each picture. Then write a word from the box next to the clue it goes with.

danger	partner

1. The cat is not safe. ____________

2. We worked together. ____________

B. Use one of the words in the box to write a sentence.

special	splendid

Name ______________________________

Context clues are words that help you figure out the meaning of a new word. When you see a new word, look for words you know to help you.

Use context clues to figure out the meaning of the word in bold. Fill in the correct circle.

1. The lions sit and **relax** on the grass.

O rest

O run

2. Lee **enjoys** seeing the lions. He has a fun time.

O likes

O looks

3. The **timid** lion hid behind his mother.

O shy

O happy

Name ______________________________

The verbs **has** and **have** mean "to own something."

We use **has** to tell about one person, place, or thing.

Clay **has** a pet.

We use **have** to tell about more than one person, place, or thing.

We also use **have** with the words **I** and **you**.

Jan and Tim **have** pet fish.

I **have** a dog.

You **have** a cat.

Circle the verb that belongs in the sentence.

1. Nick (has, have) a big dog.

2. Mike and Cal (has, have) small dogs.

3. Kim (has, have) many pretty fish.

4. I (has, have) water for the pets.

5. Zack and Lin (has, have) some cats.

6. We (has, have) a lot of fun on Pet Day.

Name ______________________________

A. Read the draft model. Find the errors.

Draft Model

James has a smal book about ants.
I has a book abowt fish.
We has fun reeding!

B. Revise the draft. Use the words <u>has</u> and <u>have</u> correctly. Make sure to spell words with long <u>e</u> correctly.

____

____

____

____

Connect to Writing

C. Look in your writer's notebook. Make sure you used <u>has</u> and <u>have</u> correctly.

Name ______________________________

Every sentence begins with a capital letter.

Every sentence ends with a period, question mark, or exclamation mark.

Example: <u>**We**</u> call my new cat Puff<u>.</u>

Write each sentence correctly.

1. what does Nan have

____

2. that chick has a small beak

____

3. it is fun to feed the animals

____

4. will the hens eat the grain

____

Ants Can Help

It is raining a lot. There is water all around. How can little ants stay safe?

Teacher Directions: Have children establish a purpose for reading the take-home story.

The raft keeps the ants safe! They can wait for the rain to stop. They may reach land. They are a good team!

Connect to Community: Have children talk to a family member about other animals or insects they know that work together.

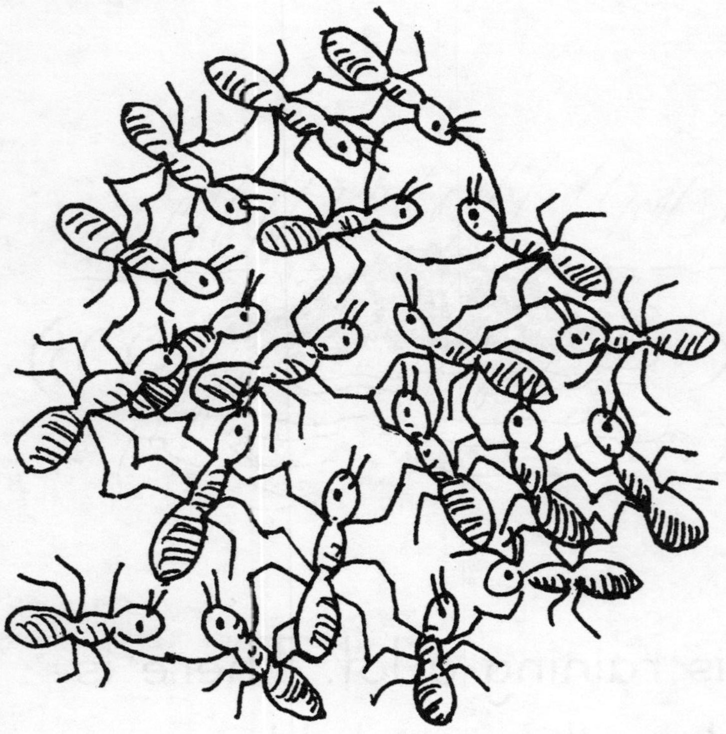

Some ants help each other. They work as a team. They get in a circle. Then they weave their legs together.

②

They make a raft. It is a raft of ants. The ants can stay on top of the water this way.

③

Name ______________________________

Look at each picture. Say the name of each picture out loud. Say the middle sounds. Circle the picture whose name has a different middle sound.

1.

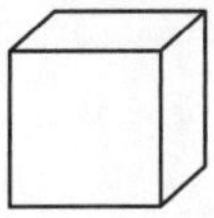

2.

3.

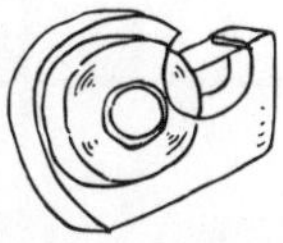

4.

5.

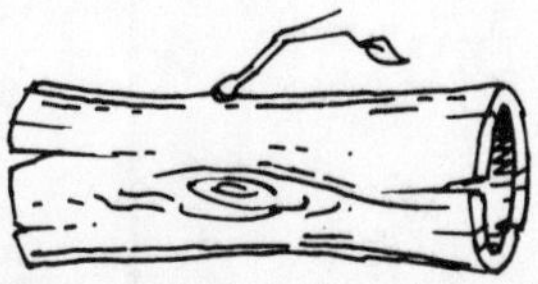

Teacher Directions: Model item 1 by saying *cube, cub,* and *run.* Repeat, stressing the difference between the long and short vowel sounds: /ū/ and /u/. Say: *The words* cub *and* run *have the same middle sound: /u/.* Cube *has a different middle sound: /ū/.* Guide children to circle the picture of the cube.

Name ____

Listen to the sounds your teacher says. Blend the sounds together. Draw a picture of the word you made.

1.	**2.**
3.	**4.**

Teacher Directions: Model item 1 by saying /b/ /ī/ /k/. *Listen as I blend these sounds together: /bīīīk/, bike.* Model drawing a bike in the first box and have children copy. For items 2–4, have children listen to the sounds and blend them to form a word. 2. Say: /b/ /ō/ /t/; 3. Say: /t/ /r/ /ā/ /n/ /s/; 4. Say: /p/ /l/ /ā/ /t/ /s/.

Name ______________________________

The letters o, oa, ow, and oe can make the long **o** sound.

go coal low doe

tow	both	hoe	coat	hold	toe	glow	road

Write the words from the box that have the same vowel sound and spelling.

1. boat  ______________ ______________

2. cold  ______________ ______________

3. doe  ______________ ______________

4. crow  ______________ ______________

Name ______________________

A. Read the words in the box. Use the words to complete the sentences.

coat	show	boat	row	toe	go

1. Put on your ______________ .

2. We can ______________ fast.

3. They put on a ______________ .

B. Add one letter to make a new word with one of the long o sounds above. Then write the word.

1. cost ______________ 2. got ______________

Name ______________________________

Fold back the paper along the dotted line. Use the blanks to write each word as it is read aloud. When you finish the test, unfold the paper. Use the list at the right to correct any spelling mistakes.

1. ____________ 1. low
2. ____________ 2. boat
3. ____________ 3. no
4. ____________ 4. row
5. ____________ 5. oat
6. ____________ 6. toe

High-Frequency Words

7. ____________ 7. over

8. ____________ 8. more

Name ______________________________

A. Read the words in the box. Then sort the words.

boat	low	no	oat	row	toe

Words with <u>ow</u>	**Words with <u>o</u>**
______________	______________
______________	______________

Words with <u>oe</u>	**Words with <u>oa</u>**
______________	______________
______________	______________

B. Think of new words to add to the chart.

Name ______________________________

A. Read the words in the box. Then sort the words.

go	low	no	oat	row	toe

Words with ow	**Words with o**
Words with oe	**Words with oa**

B. Think of new words to add to the chart.

Name ______________________________

A. Read the words in the box. Then sort the words.

boat   flow   coat   low   no   row   toe   snowman

Words with <u>ow</u>	Words with <u>o</u>	Words with <u>oe</u>	Words with <u>oa</u>

B. Think of new words to add to the chart.

Name ______________________________

low	boat	no	row	oat
toe	we	keep	over	more

A. Read the words in the box out loud. Then circle the word in each row that is spelled correctly.

1. kepe keepe keep

2. over ovur ovr

3. moore more mor

4. wie we wea

B. Write the words from the box that rhyme with grow.

5. ______________________ 6. ______________________

7. ______________________ 8. ______________________

Name ______________________________

Trace and write P and p. Copy the sentence. Make sure to leave spaces between words. Write neatly.

Pp

P P P P P P

P P P

p p p p p p p p p

p p p

Peggy pets the pup.

Name ______________________________

An **open syllable** is a syllable that ends in a vowel. It has a long vowel sound.

ro/bot **ho/tel**

Read each word. Draw a line between the syllables in each word. Write the word that has an open syllable.

1. magnet locate ______________________

2. retell escape ______________________

3. begin picnic ______________________

4. inside silent ______________________

5. sunset beneath ______________________

Name ______________________________

A. Read the sentences out loud. Then, circle the word in each sentence that has an open syllable.

1. Lissy is going to look for toys.

2. She begins looking in the toy chest.

3. She will donate the toys and help!

B. Circle the word in each group with an open syllable.

4. moment mitten rabbit

5. picnic napkin silent

C. Use one of the words you circled above to write a new sentence.

____

Name ______________________________

A. Read the words in the box out loud. Write the word from the box that completes each sentence.

find	food	more	over	start	warm

1. Give Spot some ______________ .

2. I will ______________ my coat.

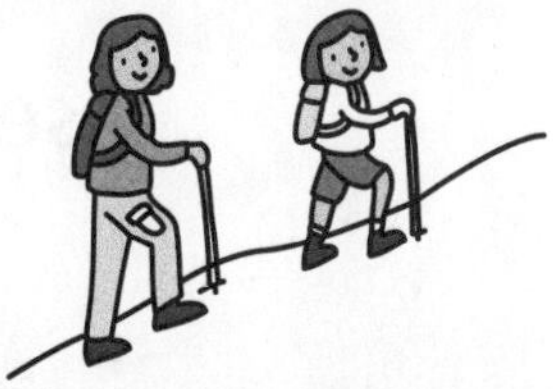

3. We hike ______________ the hill.

4. It is ______________ in the sun.

5. Jen has ______________ books.

6. ______________ the bus so we can go!

Name ________________________________

You can use the words **seek** and **search** to tell about looking for something.

Use **search** to tell about looking for something in a place.

Use **seek** to tell about looking for something you want.

A. Circle and write the word that completes the sentence.

I. Kim has to ______________ the closet for her coat.

search seek

2. The crow must ______________ out food.

search seek

B. Write a sentence using one of the words in the box.

danger partner

____

Name ______________________________

A **word category** is a group of words that are alike in some way.

Word Category: **Things People Do**

learn, eat, sleep, play

A. Write a new word to fit each category.

1. Things People Eat: bread, fruit, ____________

2. Things in Nature: trees, leaves, ____________

B. Write a category that tells how the words are alike.

Word Category:

3. wings, beak, legs, feet ____________

4. dogs, cats, birds, fish ____________

Name ______________________________

The words **go** and **do** are action verbs.

Use **go** and **do** to tell what is happening now.

Use **went** and **did** to tell what has already happened.

Present	Past
Today I **go** see Gram.	He **went** to a play last week.
We **do** our work now.	They **did** have fun last night.

A. Write the verb that tells about the present.

1. Animals ______________ a lot of work to find food.

2. Other animals ______________ in a cave to sleep.

B. Write the verb that tells about the past.

3. The ducks ______________ to a less cold place.

4. They ______________ not like the lake of ice.

Name ______________________________

A. Read the draft model. Circle the form of go or do that tells about the present. Underline any errors.

Draft Model

The todes go in the water.

Do the toads fynd any flies?

B. Revise the draft to make it past tense. Make sure to spell words with long o correctly.

____

____

____

____

Connect to Writing

C. Look in your writer's notebook. Make sure you used the words go and do correctly.

Name ______________________________

Proper nouns are the names of specific people, places, and things.

All proper nouns begin with a capital letter.

<u>J</u>ack <u>N</u>ile lives on <u>O</u>ak <u>L</u>ane.

Circle the letters that should be capital.
Write the proper nouns correctly.

1. The bus stops at west street.

______________ ______________

2. I hope mom will let me get a new pet in june.

______________ ______________

3. Did joan blake see the pets?

______________ ______________

4. We feed the ducks on blue lake.

______________ ______________

Can a crow be bold? Yes! It likes to take things. This crow brings a shell back to its nest!

Connect to Community: Have children talk to a family member about other animals they know.

④

Crows

Have you seen a crow? Crows are big. They are black birds. They live in many places.

Teacher Directions: Have children establish a purpose for reading the take-home story.

①

What does a crow eat? Crows eat what they can find. It could be ants, crops, or bugs. They even eat eggs and fish.

Crows make nests. They made this nest from sticks. The top is open.

Name ______________________________

Look at each picture. Say the name of each picture out loud. Say the middle sounds. Circle the picture whose name has a different middle sound.

1.

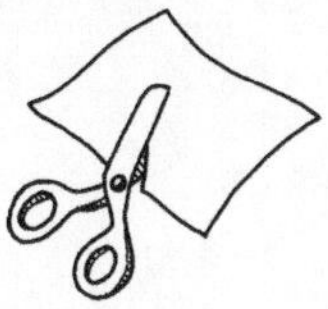

2.

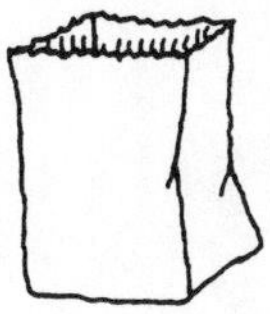
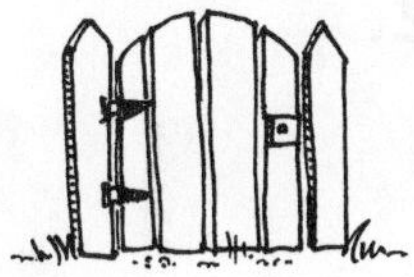

3.

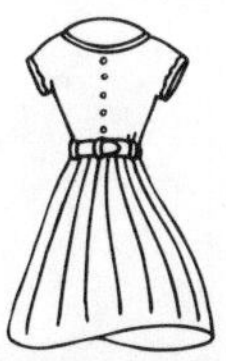

4.

5.

Teacher Directions: 1. Model: *Listen to the middle sounds of these three words:* cut, mule, *and* mug. Stress the difference between the long and short vowel sounds: /u/ and /ū/. *The words* cut *and* mug *have the same middle sound: /u/. The word* mule *has the middle sound /ū/.* Guide children to circle the picture of the mule.

Name ______________________________

Listen to the sounds your teacher says. Blend the sounds together. Circle the picture that goes with the word you made.

1.

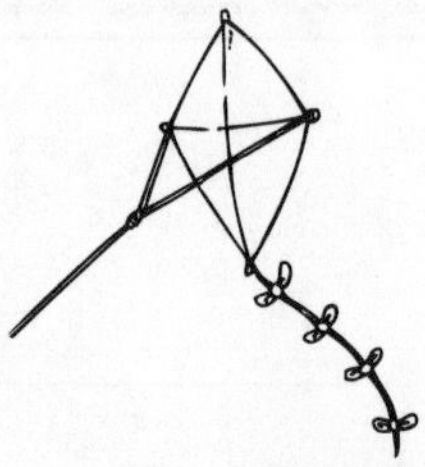

2.

3.

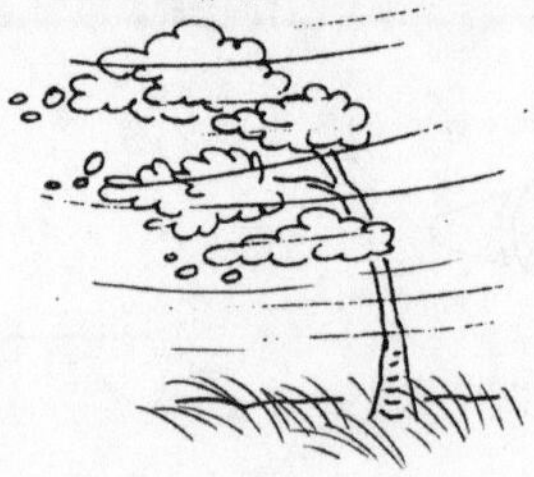

4.

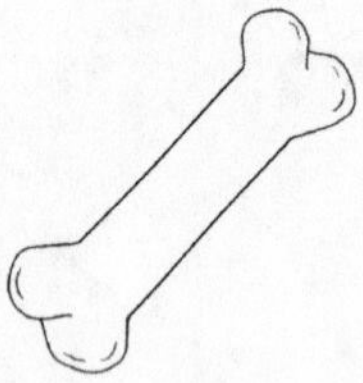

5.

Teacher Directions: Model item 1 by saying /k/ /a/ /t/. *I will blend the sounds to make a word: /kaaat/, cat.* Guide children to circle the picture of the cat for item 1. For items 2–5, say the following sounds. Have students blend the sounds to say each word. Then have them circle the picture that shows it. 2. /j/ /u/ /m/ /p/; 3. /w/ /i/ /n/ /d/; 4. /b/ /ō/ /l/; 5. /n/ /ī/ /t/.

Name ______________________________

The long **i** sound is the sound you hear in **wild**. The letters i, y, igh, and ie can make the long i sound.

find **sky** **night** **tie**

A. Read the words in ( ). Circle the long i word that completes each sentence. Write the word.

1. The baby will ____________. (cry, sips)

2. We like ____________. (cake, pie)

3. The Sun is out so there is a lot of ____________. (light, dim)

B. Write i, y, igh, or ie to complete each word.

4. w ________ l d

5. f l ________

Name ______________________________

A. Read each group of words. Circle the word in each group that has the long i sound. Write the word.

1.	ring	rip	right	______
2.	twist	tie	thin	______
3.	child	chill	chip	______
4.	drip	dry	dig	______
5.	mist	mitt	might	______

B. Add two letters to make a new word with the long i sound. Then write the word.

1. sit ______________ 2. lit ______________

Name ____________________

Fold back the paper along the dotted line. Use the blanks to write each word as it is read aloud. When you finish the test, unfold the paper. Use the list at the right to correct any spelling mistakes.

1. ____________________ **1. find**

2. ____________________ **2. night**

3. ____________________ **3. by**

4. ____________________ **4. kind**

5. ____________________ **5. right**

6. ____________________ **6. pie**

High-Frequency Words

7. ____________________ **7. caught**

8. ____________________ **8. listen**

Name ________________________________

A. Read the words in the box. Then sort the words.

by	find	right	pie	night	kind

Words with <u>igh</u>	Words with <u>y</u>
____________	____________
____________	____________

Words with <u>ie</u>	Words with <u>i</u>
____________	____________
____________	____________

B. Think of new words to add to the chart.

Name ____________________

A. Read the words in the box. Then sort the words.

by find high kind night pie

Words with igh	Words with y

Words with ie	Words with i

B. Think of new words to add to the chart.

Name ______________________________

A. Read the words in the box. Then sort the words.

by	dried	find	my
night	kind	right	pie

Words with igh	Words with y
____________	____________
____________	____________
____________	____________

Words with ie	Words with i
____________	____________
____________	____________
____________	____________

B. Think of new words to add to the chart.

Name ______________________________

Choose a letter or spelling pattern from the box to complete each spelling word. Then write the word.

y	oa	igh	i	ie

1. k ____ nd ______________

2. b ____ ______________

3. b ____ ____ t ______________

4. n ____ ____ ____ t ______________

5. p ____ ____ ______________

Name ______________________________

Trace and write Z and z. Then copy the sentence. Make sure to leave spaces between words. Write neatly.

Z Z Z Z Z Z

Z Z Z

z z z z z z z z

z z z

Zeke zips his zipper.

Name ______________________________

To add the ending -**es** or -**ed** to a word that ends with long **i** spelled **y**, first change the **y** to **i**.

dry + es = dries **dry + ed = dried**

Do not change the **y** to **i** when adding -**ing**.

dry + ing = drying

Add the ending. Write the new word. Read the word you made out loud.

1. cry + es = ______________________________

2. try + ed = ______________________________

3. spy + es = ______________________________

4. fly + ing = ______________________________

Name ______________________________

A. Circle the word that completes each sentence. Then read each sentence.

1. I am (trying, trieng) to win the game.

2. The baby (cryed, cried) a lot.

3. The plane (flys, flies) high in the sky.

B. Add the ending to the word. Write the new word.

4. fry + ing = ______________________

5. try + es = ______________________

C. Use one of the words you circled or wrote above to write a new sentence.

____

____

____

Name ______________________________

Read the words in the box out loud. Write the word from the box that completes each sentence.

caught	flew	know	laugh	listen	were

1. The butterfly ______________ away.

2. They ______________ playing in mud.

3. He ______________ a bug.

4. I ______________ at jokes.

5. We must ______________ in school.

6. Do you ______________ where bees live?

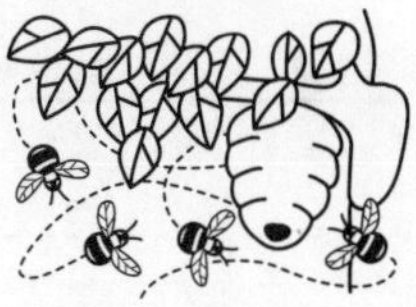

Name ______________________________

A. Write a sentence that uses the word <u>beautiful</u>. Then draw a picture to go with your sentence.

B. Write a sentence that uses the word <u>fancy</u>.

C. Write a sentence that uses the word <u>search</u>.

Name ______________________________

Context clues are words that help you figure out the meaning of a new word. Look for context clues in the same sentence or in nearby sentences.

Use context clues to figure out the meaning of the word in bold. Fill in the circle next to the word's meaning.

1. There are many kinds of bugs, but all **insects** have six legs.

○ bugs

○ legs

2. Most spiders are **harmless** and won't hurt you.

○ safe

○ dangerous

3. Some caterpillars have **bristles**, or short hairs.

○ eyes

○ hairs

Name ______________________________

Use **see** when looking at something now.

I see the bugs. **You see** the bugs.

We see the bugs. **They see** the bugs.

Use **sees** when **he** or **she** is looking now.

She sees the bugs. **Joe sees** the bugs.

Use **saw** to tell about looking in the past.

Last week we **saw** the bugs.

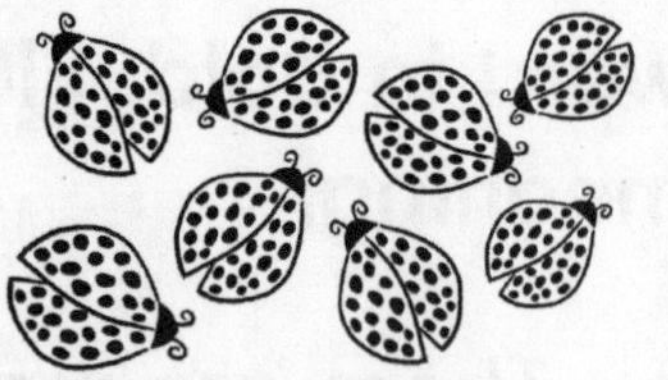

A. Circle the verb that tells about the present.

1. Blake (see, sees, saw) a small ant.

2. Joe and Tate (see, sees, saw) some bees.

3. I (see, sees, saw) a bug on a leaf.

B. Circle the verb that tells about the past.

4. Last week we (see, sees, saw) a flea.

5. Matt (see, sees, saw) a white moth.

6. Jess and Nan (see, sees, saw) a tan snail.

Name ______________________________

A. Read the draft model. Circle the verbs in the past tense. Underline the errors.

Draft Model

Kim saw a bluu bird.

She saw it flie above the trees.

B. Change the sentences to be in the present tense. Make sure to spell words with long i correctly. Rewrite the sentences below.

____

____

____

____

Connect to Writing

C. Look in your writer's notebook. Check that you used see and saw correctly.

Name ______________________________

Use **see** and **sees** to tell about the present. Use **saw** to tell about the past. Underline book titles.

Circle the mistake in each sentence.
Write the sentence correctly on the line.

1. I sees a tan bug.

____

2. Last week Mom see a snail on the ledge.

____

3. I will read All About Bugs to find out more.

____

4. I will get a new book, A Snail's Pail, today.

____

Eve and Pete slept in the tree. Then one day, the bugs woke up. It was warm! So Eve and Pete left the tree. They flew up to the sky.

Connect to Community: Have children talk to a family member about what they do when it's cold outside.

Eve and Pete

Eve and Pete were pals.
They flew and flew high and low.
They had so much fun together.

Teacher Directions: Have children establish a purpose for reading the take-home story.

Then one day, Pete said, "It's getting cold. We need to find a tree. We need to sleep."

"Let's look for one," said Eve.

②

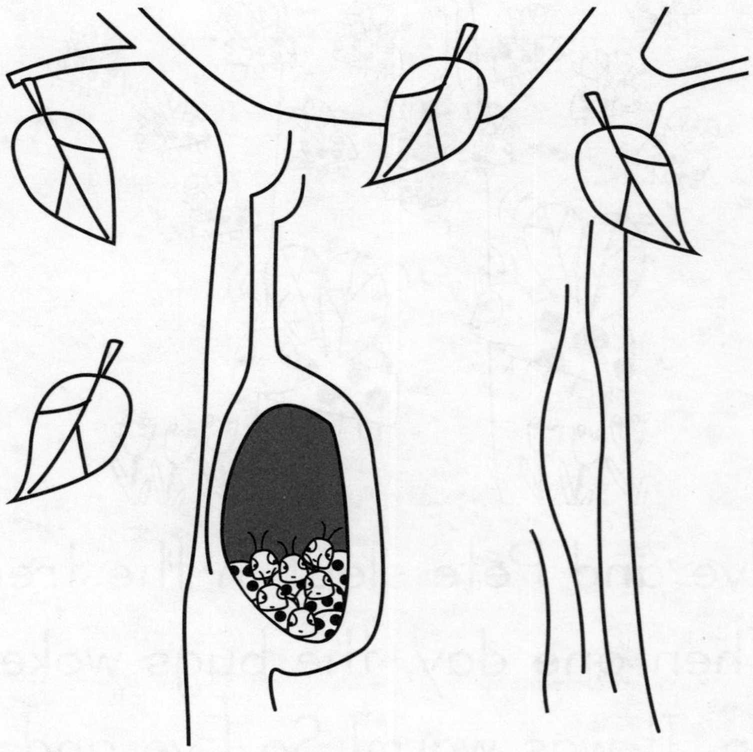

They spotted a huge tree. There were lots of bugs in it.

"Hi! Stay with us," the bugs cried. "You will be warm here."

③

Name ______________________________

Look at each picture. Say the name of each picture out loud. Say the middle sounds. Circle the picture whose name has a different middle sound.

1.

2.

3.

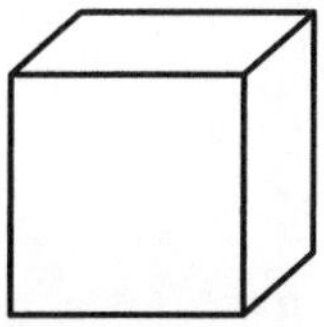

4.

5.

Teacher Directions: Model item I by saying *rat, cat,* and *vase*. Repeat, stressing the difference between the long and short vowel sounds: /a/ and /ā/. Say: *The words* rat *and* cat *have the same middle sound: /a/.* Vase *has a different middle sound: /ā/.* Guide children to circle the picture of the vase.

Name ____

Listen to each word your teacher says. Take away the sound. Circle the picture of the new word you made.

1.

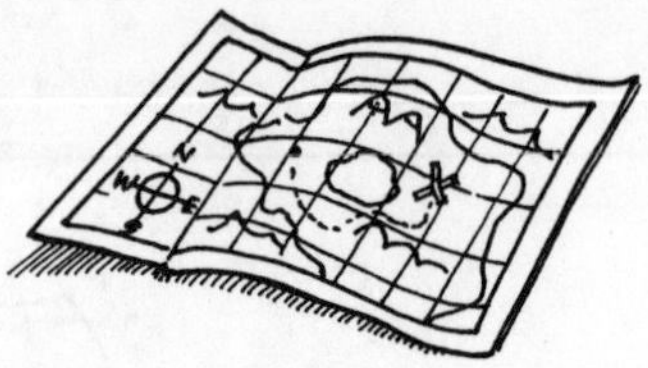

2.

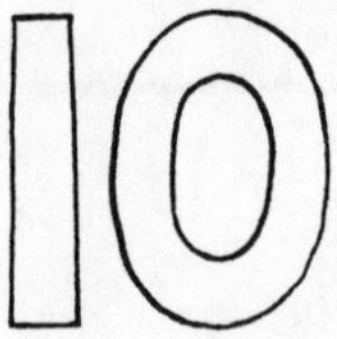

3.

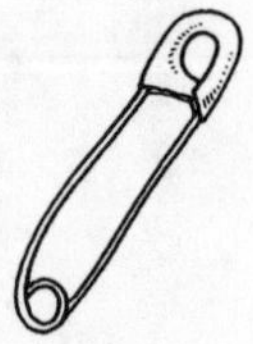

4.

5.

Teacher Directions: Explain to children that we can take away a sound from a word to make a new word. Model item 1 by saying *mend. I can take away /d/ from the ending of mend to make a new word: /mmmeeennn/,* men. Guide children to circle the picture of the men. 2. Say *tent.* Tell children to take away /t/ from the ending of *tent.* 3. Say *pink.* Tell children to take away /k/ from the ending of *pink.* 4. Say *tint.* Tell children to take away /t/ from the ending of *tint.* 5. Say *wind.* Tell children to take away /d/ from the ending of *wind.*

Name ____________________

The letters y and ey at the end of a word can make the long **e** sound.

baby **valley**

Write y or ey on the line. Then write the word.

1.  k ______ ____________________

2. 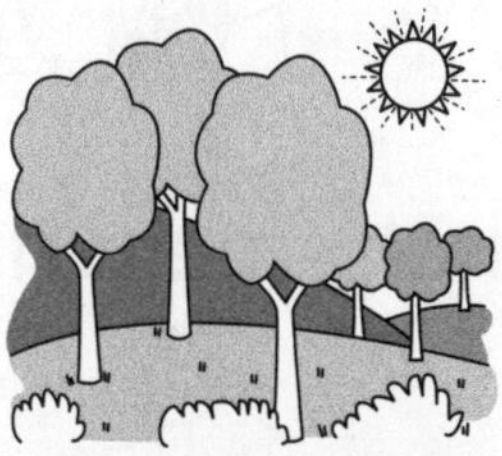 sunn ______ ____________________

3.  cit ______ ____________________

4.  lad ______ ____________________

Name ______________________________

A. Use the words in the box to complete the sentences.

easy	money	happy	tidy	honey

1. It's not ____________________ to clean our dog!

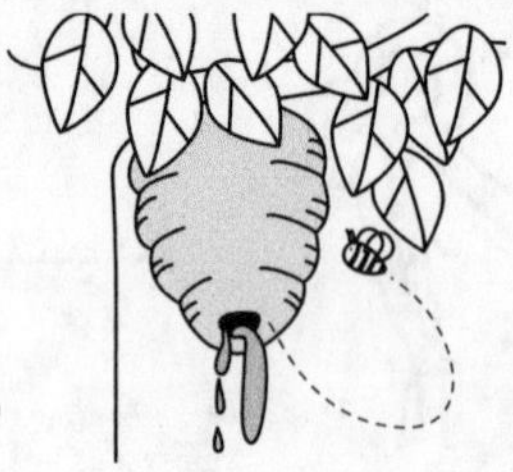

2. Bees make ____________________.

3. I am ____________________ that you can help me write.

4. My desk is neat and ____________________.

B. Add one letter to make a new word with the long e sound spelled y. Then write the word.

1. box ____________________ 2. bell ____________________

Name ______________________________

Fold back the paper along the dotted line. Use the blanks to write each word as it is read aloud. When you finish the test, unfold the paper. Use the list at the right to correct any spelling mistakes.

1. ____________	1. key
2. ____________	2. bumpy
3. ____________	3. puppy
4. ____________	4. funny
5. ____________	5. penny
6. ____________	6. sandy
7. ____________	7. wash
8. ____________	8. would

High-Frequency Words

Name ____________________

A. Read the words in the box. Then sort the words.

bumpy funny key penny puppy sandy

Words with <u>ey</u>	Words with <u>y</u>

B. Think of new words to add to the chart.

Name ______________________________

A. Read the words in the box. Then sort the words.

funny happy key penny puppy sunny

Words with <u>ey</u>	Words with <u>y</u>

B. Think of new words to add to the chart.

Name ______________________________

A. Read the words in the box. Then sort the words.

bumpy bunny funny key monkey penny puppy sandy

Words with ey	Words with y

B. Think of new words to add to the chart.

Name ______________________________

key	bumpy	puppy	funny	penny
sandy	my	night	wash	would

Read the words in the box. Then look at each set of words. One word in each set is spelled correctly. Use a pencil to fill in the circle in front of that word.

1. ○ night
○ nite
○ nitte

2. ○ penney
○ peny
○ penny

3. ○ funni
○ funny
○ funey

4. ○ kee
○ kie
○ key

5. ○ sandey
○ sandy
○ sandee

6. ○ my
○ mai
○ mey

7. ○ bumpee
○ bumpey
○ bumpy

8. ○ wud
○ would
○ woud

Name ______________________________

Trace and write M and m. Then copy the sentence. Make sure to leave spaces between words.

M M M M M M M

M M M

m m m m m m m m m

m m m

Meg made my meal.

Name ________________________________

A **compound word** is made up of smaller words. Read each smaller word. Then read the compound word.

rain + coat = raincoat

A. Add a word from the box to a word below to make a compound word. Write the word from the box. Then read the compound word.

walk	time	work	book

1. home ____________

2. note ____________

3. side ____________

4. lunch ____________

B. Circle the compound word. Then draw a line between the two smaller words. Then say the words out loud.

5. someone singing

6. silly inside

Name ______________________________

A. Read each of the smaller words in the compound words in ( ). Then circle the word that completes each sentence.

1. Dad tells me when it is (notebook, bedtime).

2. We play in the Sun (outside, inside).

3. Pam does (sidewalk, homework) at 4:00.

B. Circle the compound word. Then draw a line between the two smaller words. Then say the words out loud.

4. backpack unpack

5. basket baseball

C. Use one of the words you circled above to write a new sentence.

____

____

____

Name ______________________________

Read the words in the box out loud. Write a word from the box to complete each sentence.

found	hard	near	woman	would	write

1. It can be ____________________ to wake up.

2. Jen ____________________ her coat.

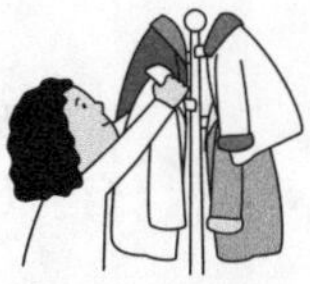

3. Ed is ____________________ the top.

4. ____________________ you like a berry?

5. We ____________________ in class.

6. Ms. Smith is a ____________________ .

Name ______________________

A person who is **clever** thinks of good ideas quickly.

The clever girl found the answer to the riddle.

If you see or hear a **signal**, it is time to do something.

A teacher will give a signal to line up for gym class.

A. Write clever or signal to complete each sentence.

1. Kim gave a ______________ to Ted.

2. The ______________ bear found the honey.

3. Class begins at the ______________ of the bell.

B. Write your own sentence using the word beautiful.

____

____

Name ______________________________

A **base word** is a word that can stand alone. You can add letters to a base word to make a new word.

look + ed = looked **look + ing = looking**

look + s = looks

When you see a new word, look for a base word to help you figure out the meaning.

Read the word. Underline the base word. Then match the word to the picture.

1. filling
2. spilled
3. giving
4. opened
5. cooks

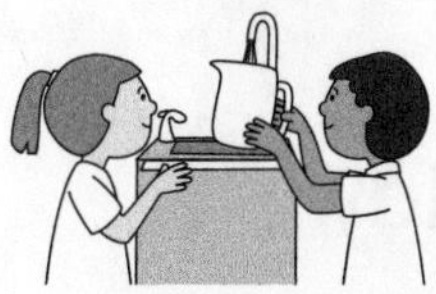

Name ________________________________

An **adverb** is a word that tells more about a verb in a sentence.

A verb tells about action.

An adverb can tell when an action happened.

Examples: Tim ran a race **today**.

today ⟶ tells when Tim ran a race

Read the sentences. Underline the adverbs that tell when.

1. Gram will come to see me soon.
2. My dad hit a home run yesterday.
3. Now I can ride my bike.
4. We will have lunch next.
5. Then we will go out to play.
6. Today I am going to ride the bus.

Name ___________________________________

A. Read the draft model. Find the errors.

Draft Model

Tom fownd a puppey.

His mom helped him find the pup's home.

B. Now revise the draft. Add adverbs that tell when to each sentence. Rewrite the sentences below.

Connect to Writing

C. Look in your writer's notebook. Check that you used adverbs correctly.

Name ______________________________

When you write three verbs in a list, put a **comma** after the first two verbs.

Example: The sheep eat, drink, and graze all day.

↑ ↑ commas

Put commas in the sentences where they belong.

1. I wash rinse and dry the cups.

2. We like to swim splash and dive in the pool.

3. We mix bake and eat the cupcakes.

4. We walk jog and run in the park.

5. Gram and I dig plant and water.

Hold a treat near the puppy's nose. Then say, "Sit!" Do it many times. What will the puppy do? It just might sit!

Connect to Community: Have children talk to a family member about what type of pet they would like.

4

A New Puppy

Would you like a puppy? You can find one here. They are all so cute. The woman can help you pick the right one.

Teacher Directions: Have children establish a purpose for reading the take-home story.

1

You find a puppy. Now you bring it home. Having a puppy is hard work. Why? You must train it. It is not easy.

2

You can take it to school or train it at home. What can you train the puppy to do? You can teach it to sit.

3

Name ________________________________

Listen to the middle sounds in **coat** and **dog**. They are different.

The middle sounds in **red** and **hen** are the same.

Say the name of each picture out loud. Circle the picture whose name has a different middle sound.

1.

2.

3.

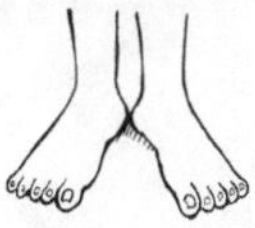

4.

5.

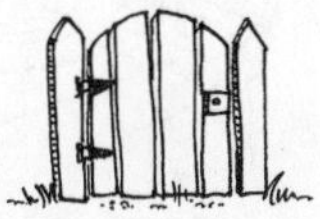

Teacher Directions: Read the box at the top of the page. Point to the pictures as you say *coat* and *dog.* Stress the difference in vowel sounds. The point to the pictures as you say *red* and *hen.* Again, stress the middle sounds.

Name ______________________________

Look at first picture in each row. Say the name of each picture out loud. Circle the picture whose name has the same middle sound as the first picture.

1. 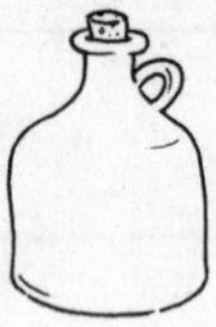		
2. 		
3. 	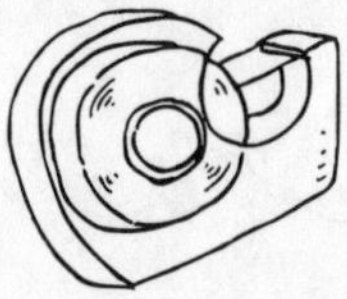	
4. 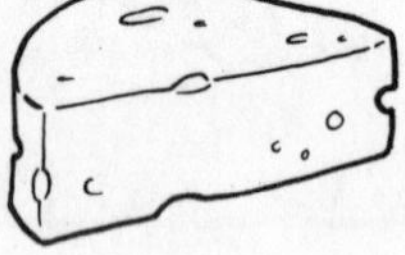		
5. 		

Teacher Directions: Model item 1 by saying *jug, pup,* and *mule*. Repeat, stressing the difference between the long and short vowel sounds: /u/ and /ū/. Say: *The words* jug *and* pup *have the same middle sound: /u/.* Mule *has a different middle sound: /ū/.* Guide children to circle the picture of the pup.

Name ______________________________

The letters ar together make the sound you hear at the end of **car**.

A. Read the words in the box. Listen for the ar sounds. Write the word that names each picture.

scarf	arm	shark	star

1. ____________ 

2. ____________ 

3. ____________ 

4. ____________ 

B. Write your own sentence using a word from the box.

____

____

Name ______________________________

A. Circle and write the word that completes the sentence.

1. The ducks and hens live on a ______________.

far farm

2. A ______________ can swim fast.

shark sharp

3. I got a ______________ in the mail today.

card car

4. I saw a pig near the ______________.

barn bark

B. Add one letter to make a new word with the sound you hear in car. Then write the word.

1. had ______________ 2. cat ______________

Name ______________________________

Fold back the paper along the dotted line. Use the blanks to write each word as it is read aloud. When you finish the test, unfold the paper. Use the list at the right to correct any spelling mistakes.

1. ______________ 1. cart

2. ______________ 2. barn

3. ______________ 3. arm

4. ______________ 4. art

5. ______________ 5. yarn

6. ______________ 6. harm

High-Frequency Words

7. ______________ 7. four

8. ______________ 8. none

Name ______________________________

A. Read the words in the box. Then sort the words using the word endings.

arm	art	barn	cart	harm	yarn

Words with arn	Words with arm	Words with art

B. Think of words that have the same word endings. Add them to the chart.

Name ______________________________

A. Read the words in the box. Then sort the words.

arm	art	barn	car	far	harm

Words with arn	**Words with art**
____________	____________
____________	____________
Words with arm	**Words with ar**
____________	____________
____________	____________

B. Think of words that have the same word endings. Add them to the chart.

Name ______________________________

A. Read the words in the box. Then sort the words.

arm	art	barn	cart	chart	harm	smart	yarn

Words with <u>arn</u>	**Words with <u>arm</u>**	**Words with <u>art</u>**

B. Think of new words to add to the chart.

Name ______________________________

cart	barn	arm	art	yarn
harm	happy	key	four	none

Write the spelling word that names the picture.

1. ____________________

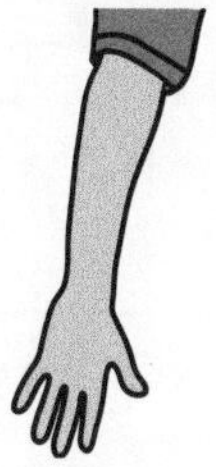

2. ____________________

3. ____________________

4. ____________________

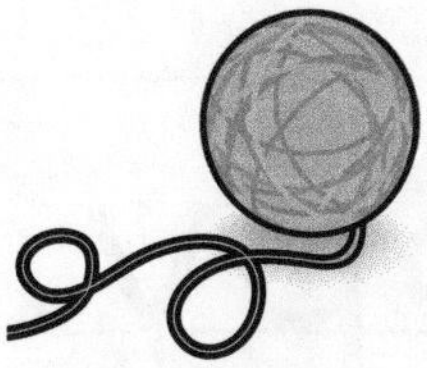

5. ____________________

6. ____________________

Name ____________________

Trace and write H and h. Then copy the sentence.
Make sure to leave spaces between words. Write neatly.

Hh

H H H H H H

H H H

h h h h h h h h h

h h h

Henry is happy.

Name ______________________________

If a noun ends in a consonant followed by -y, first change the y to i. Then add es to make it plural.

penny + es = pennies **city + es = cities**

Add the ending. Write the new word. Read the word you made out loud.

1. baby + es = ______________

2. story + es = ______________

3. berry + es = ______________

4. lady + es = ______________

5. cherry + es = ______________

Name ______________________________

A. Circle the word that completes each sentence. Then read the sentence out loud.

1. We had blue (skys, skies) this week.

2. She read two (stories, storyes) at school.

3. Pam and Ted live in different (citys, cities).

B. Add the ending to the word. Write the new word.

4. country + es = ____________________

5. duty + es = ____________________

C. Use one of the words you circled or wrote above to write a new sentence.

____

____

____

Name ______________________________

Read the words in the box out loud. Complete each sentence. Use one of the words in the box.

four	none	only	large	put	round

1. That shark is ______________ !

2. Carl wants an apple, but there are ______________ .

3. The shape of this cake is ______________ .

4. I see ______________ one cat here.

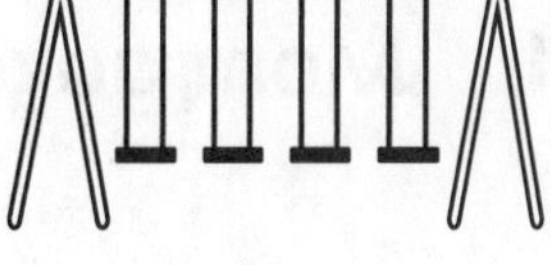

5. There are ______________ swings.

6. I can help ______________ the dishes in the sink.

Name ______________________________

trouble: If you have <u>trouble</u> doing something, you have problems doing it.

whole: When something is <u>whole</u>, it is complete. None of it is missing.

A. Match each sentence to the picture that it tells about.

1. I had trouble cleaning my room.

2. We will eat the whole cake.

a. 

b. 

B. Complete each sentence. Use the word <u>clever</u> or <u>signal</u>.

1. Mom gave us a ____________ to wait to cross the street.

2. The ____________ dog found the treats.

Name ____

Some words have more than one meaning.

bark part of a tree

bark a sound a dog makes

My dog likes to **bark** at trucks.

The word **dog** is a clue to help you know the correct meaning of **bark** in this sentence.

Read each sentence. Fill in the circle next to the picture that shows the correct meaning of the bold word. Use other words in the sentence to help you.

1. We will see a **play** today.

Ⓐ 

Ⓑ 

2. I **left** my lunch on the seat of the bus.

Ⓐ 

Ⓑ 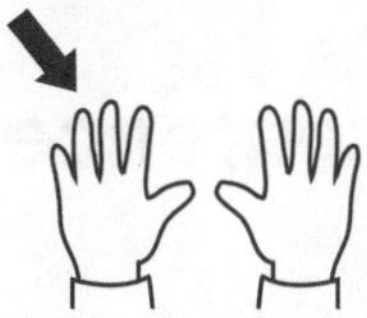

3. Let's **seal** the box and then mail it.

Ⓐ 

Ⓑ 

Name ______________________________

Two sentences can be joined together. Use the words **and, but,** and **or** with a comma to combine sentences.

Example: Kyle had a snack**, and** Max ate lunch.

A cause and effect can be joined using **so** or **because**.

Cause: Helen waters the plants.

Effect: The plants will grow.

Helen waters the plants, **so** the plants will grow.

A. Circle the word used to join the two sentences.

1. I like to run, and I like to jump.
2. Can Ella come to my party, or can Lily come?
3. Kim rides a bike, but Brad rides a scooter.

B. Combine the sentences using so or because.

1. Callie's mom got a new car. Her old one broke.

____

Name ______________________________

A. Read the draft model. Find the errors.

Draft Model

My fore friends like the purk. It is raining. Should we play in the park? Should we stay inside?

B. Combine the sentences. Use the words <u>and</u>, <u>or</u>, and <u>but</u>. Use commas correctly. Fix any errors.

____

____

____

____

____

____

____

Connect to Writing

C. Look in your writer's notebook. Make sure you used <u>and</u>, <u>or</u>, and <u>but</u> correctly.

Name ______________________________

And, but, and **or** are words used to combine sentences.

Special place names begin with capital letters.

Example: Rachel went to Long Beach **and** she had fun.

Draw a circle around the words that combine the sentences. Draw a line under the words that should begin with a capital letter.

1. Val can take a music class, or she can take an art class.

2. Ann lives in new jersey, and her cousins live in texas.

3. Peter wanted to pick pumpkins, but applegate farm was closed.

4. We can go camping at hudson park, or we can go fishing at highland lake.

5. Gina had lunch at the tip top diner, and her best pal came with her.

Then the pals went for a swim. "You are great pals!" said Cat. They had fun, fun, fun in the sun!

Connect to Community: Have children talk to a family member about a time they had fun with their friends.

The Party

"I am six today," laughed Cat.

"Let's have a party."

"Let's have it at the beach," said her pals. "It is not far."

Teacher Directions: Have children establish a purpose for reading the take-home story.

"I will bring hats!," said Pig.
"I will bake a cake!" said Dog.
"I will make a gift and card!"
said Chick.

②

The four pals went to the beach.
They put on party hats.
They ate cake. Cat opened her gift and card.

③

Name ____

Words that rhyme end with the same sounds.

cat bat hat

Say each picture name. Then draw two pictures of things whose names rhymes with it.

1. 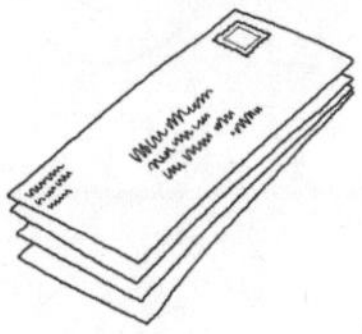		
2. 		
3. 		
4. 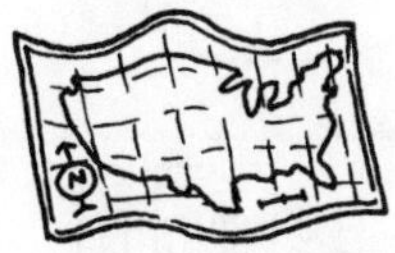		
5. 		

Teacher Directions: Read the box at the top of the page. Point to the pictures as you say *cat, bat,* and *hat*. Emphasize the ending in each word. Point out that all three words rhyme.

Name ______________________________

Listen to the word your teacher says. Replace the sound. Circle the picture of the new word you made.

1.

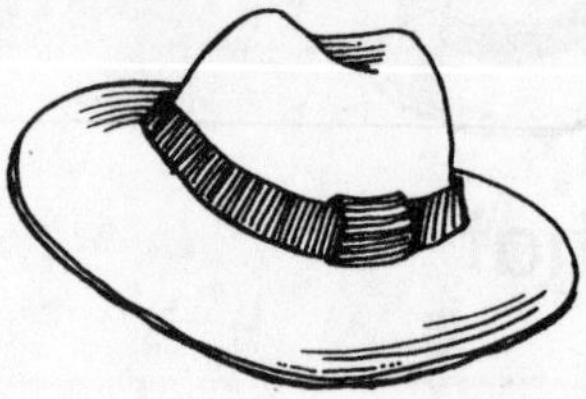

2.

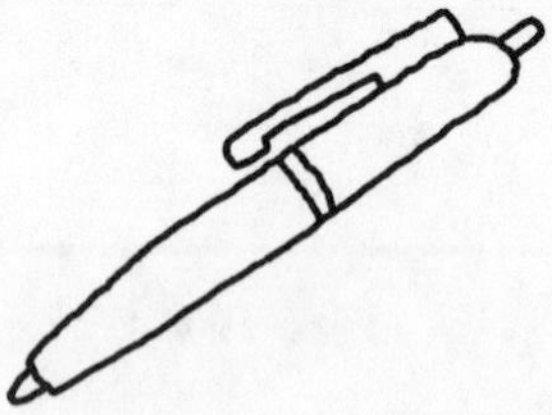

3.

4.

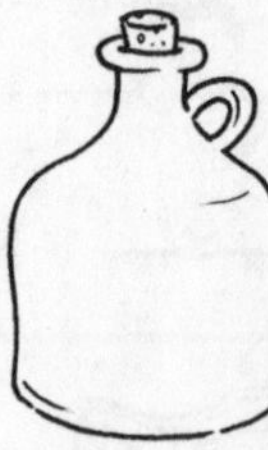

5.

Teacher Directions: 1. Model: This is the picture for the word *hat. I can change the middle sound /a/ to /i/ to make a new word. Listen to the new word:* hit. Circle the picture for the word *hit.* 2. Say *pen.* Replace the /n/ sound with /t/. 3. Say *hot.* Replace the /o/ sound with /u/. 4. Say *bug.* Replace the /b/ sound with /h/. 5. Say *crab.* Replace the /a/ sound with /i/.

Name ______________________________

The end sound you hear in **fur** can be spelled **er** as in **her**, **ir** as in **dirt**, **ur** as in **turn**, and **or** as in **word**.

A. Read the words. Listen for the sound at the end of fur. Circle the word that names the picture.

1. bed   bird 
2. wide   worm 

B. Use a word from the box to complete each sentence.

her	nurse	skirt	work

3. There is a ______________ at my school.

4. ______________ hat is green.

5. I have a pretty blue ______________.

Name ______________________________

A. Circle the word that completes the sentence. Write the word. Then read the sentence out loud.

1. Nan ______________ her foot.

   hut   hurt

2. The bird will eat the ______________.

   wave   worm

3. The ______________ is in the nest.

   bag   bird

B. Add one letter to make a new word with the sound you hear at the end of <u>fur</u>. Then write the word.

1. cub ______________   2. bun ______________

Name ______________________________

Fold back the paper along the dotted line. Use the blanks to write each word as it is read aloud. When you finish the test, unfold the paper. Use the list at the right to correct any spelling mistakes.

1. ________________ 1. her
2. ________________ 2. bird
3. ________________ 3. fur
4. ________________ 4. fern
5. ________________ 5. dirt
6. ________________ 6. work

High-Frequency Words

7. ________________ 7. climb
8. ________________ 8. through

Name ______________________________

A. Read the words in the box. Then sort the words.

bird	dirt	fern	fur	her	work

Words with er	Words with ir
______________	______________
______________	______________

Words with or	Words with ur
______________	______________
______________	______________

B. Think of new words to add to the chart.

Name ______________________________

A. Read the words in the box. Then sort the words.

bird	dirt	fur	her	turn	work

Words with <u>er</u>	Words with <u>ir</u>

Words with <u>or</u>	Words with <u>ur</u>

B. Think of new words to add to the chart.

Name ______________________________

A. Read the words in the box. Then sort the words.

bird burn dirt fern fur her work world

Words with <u>er</u>	**Words with <u>ir</u>**
______________	______________
______________	______________
______________	______________
Words with <u>or</u>	**Words with <u>ur</u>**
______________	______________
______________	______________
______________	______________

B. Think of new words to add to the chart.

Name ________________________________

her	bird	fur	fern	dirt
work	barn	arm	climb	through

A. Change one letter to write the spelling word correctly.

1. hir ____________ **2.** durt ____________

3. firn ____________ **4.** fer ____________

5. werk ____________ **6.** burd ____________

B. Circle and write the word that is spelled correctly.

7. arrm arme arm ____________

8. through throuhg thrugh ____________

Name ______________________________

Trace and write K and k. Then copy the sentence. Make sure to leave spaces between words. Write neatly.

Kk

K K K K K K

K K K

k k k k k k k k

k k k

Kenny keeps the key.

Name ______________________________

Adding -**er** to an action word changes the word to a naming word.

teach + **er** = **teacher** — a person who teaches

work + **er** = **worker** — a person who works

Add -er to the action word to make a naming word. Write and read the new word.

1. paint + er = ______________________

2. help + er = ______________________

3. play + er = ______________________

4. surf + er = ______________________

Name ____________________

A. Circle the word that completes each sentence. Then read each sentence.

1. My (teacher, teaches) helps me with the test.

2. The (surfing, surfer) rides the wave.

3. The (farmers, farms) work on the crops.

B. Add -er to the action word to make it a naming word. Write the new word.

4. kick + er = ____________________

5. send + er = ____________________

C. Use one of the words you circled or wrote above to write a new sentence.

____

Name ______________________________

Read the words in the box out loud. Draw a line to match the sentence to the picture it describes.

1. Can I have **another** cup of water?

a. 

2. My bag is **full** of food.

b. 

3. The boy will **climb** up the tree.

c. 

4. We walk **through** the door at school.

d. 

5. The **poor** girl is sick.

e. 

6. That kite is **great**.

f. 

Name ______________________________

Leaped means to have jumped far.

Stretched means to have extended a body part.

A. Use a word from the box to finish each sentence.

leaped	stretched

1. Millie ________________ her arms to her mom.

2. The frog ________________ across the pond.

B. Write a sentence using a word from the box below.

trouble	whole

____

Name ____________________

Shades of meaning are small differences in meaning between similar words.

Read the sentences. Then choose the best word in bold to answer the question.

1. Max is very wet. Is Max **soaked** or **damp**?

____

2. Tess is giving the dog some food.
Is Tess **pouring** or **spilling** the food?

____

3. Kate thinks the party is great.
Does Kate think the party is **good** or **wonderful**?

____

Name ______________________________

An **adjective** tells number, color, size, shape, and how things look, feel, smell, or taste.

Examples: We ate **red** apples for lunch.

Mark ate **two little** apples.

An **adjective** is a word that tells about a noun.
A noun names a person, place, or thing.

Example: I looked at the pretty flowers.

adjective noun

Circle the adjective in each sentence. Underline the noun it tells about.

1. Ruff is a shaggy dog.

2. Michael is wearing blue shorts.

3. I ate a sweet apple for a snack.

4. Kim likes her warm coat.

5. We flew our kite on a windy day.

Name ______________________________

A. Read the draft model. Circle the errors.

Draft Model

Kathy lieks to clime the slide.

There are burds in the yard.

Kathy smells flowers.

B. Now revise the draft. Add adjectives to each sentence. Fix the errors you found. Rewrite the sentences below.

____

____

____

____

Connect to Writing

C. Look in your writer's notebook. Make sure you used adjectives correctly.

Name ____

Adjectives tell number, color, size, or shape.

Adjectives also tell how things look, sound, feel, smell, or taste.

All sentences end with an end mark.

Read each sentence. Circle each adjective. Write the correct end mark on the line.

1. I am cleaning my messy room ________

2. I see a big spider ________

3. Why is it on the green chair ________

4. I'll call my little sister for help ________

5. The black spider ran for her life ________

"That wishing star worked," said Bethy. She put on her hat.

"It's my turn next," said Freddy.

"Good!" said Bethy.

Connect to Community: Have children talk to a family member about something they would wish for on a wishing star.

4

A Bunny Wish

"There's a wishing star!" Bethy Bunny said to Freddy Frog. "I wish for a sun hat!" They were going to the beach the next day.

Teacher Directions: Have children establish a purpose for reading the take-home story.

1

"I think you will get your wish," said Freddy Frog.
"I think I will, too," said Bethy.

2

The next day Freddy gave Bethy a sun hat.
"I got my wish!" exclaimed Bethy.

3

Name ______________________________

Look at each picture. Say the name of each picture out loud. Say the middle sounds. Circle the picture whose name has a different middle sound.

1.   

2.   

3.   

4.   

5.   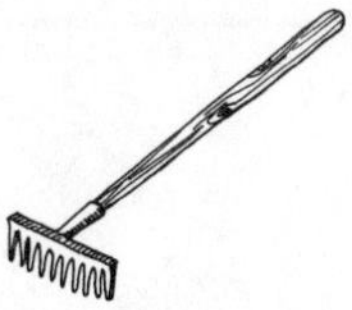

Teacher Directions: Model item 1 by saying *wag, wave,* and *van.* Repeat, stressing the difference between the long and short vowel sounds: /a/ and /ā/. Say: *The words* wag *and* van *have the same middle sound: /a/.* Wave *has a different middle sound: /ā/.* Guide children to circle the picture of the wave.

Name ______________________________

Listen to the word your teacher says. Replace the sound. Circle the picture of the new word you made.

1.			
2.		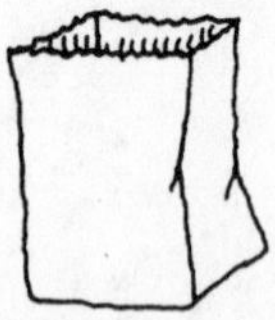	
3.			
4.		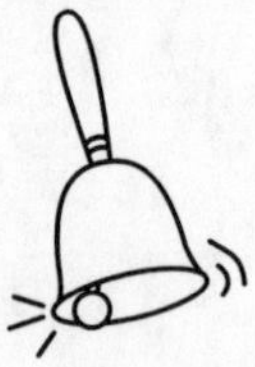	
5.			

Teacher Directions: I. Model: *This is the picture for the word* fan. *I can change the middle sound /a/ to /i/ to make a new word. Listen to the new word:* fin. Circle the picture for the word *fin.* 2. Say *wig.* Replace the /w/ sound with /p/. 3. Say *dog.* Replace the /o/ sound with /i/. 4. Say *bed.* Replace the /e/ sound with /u/. 5. Say *cab.* Replace the /b/ sound with /t/.

Name ______________________________

The letters or, ore, and oar make the sound you hear in **for**, **more**, and **board**.

Circle the word that answers the riddle. Then underline the letters that spell the or sounds as in for, more, or board.

1. I put on my hat.
   What did I do? give wore

2. You need to buy things.
   Where do you go? store star

3. We go out and see new things.
   What do we do? explore bore

4. There is rain and wind!
   What is it? storm steam

5. Leo spoke!
   What did Leo do? fetch roar

Name ______________________________

A. Read the words in the box. Use the words in the box to complete the sentences. Then read the sentences.

chore	porch	sport	roar	adore

I. Max and Bev ______________ puppies.

2. Taking out the trash is my ______________.

3. Baseball is a fun ______________.

B. Add one letter to make a new word with the sound you hear in <u>for</u>, <u>more</u>, and <u>board</u>. Then write the word.

I. pot ______________ 2. shot ______________

Name ______________________________

Fold back the paper along the dotted line. Use the blanks to write each word as it is read aloud. When you finish the test, unfold the paper. Use the list at the right to correct any spelling mistakes.

1. ____________ 1. born
2. ____________ 2. corn
3. ____________ 3. core
4. ____________ 4. more
5. ____________ 5. roar
6. ____________ 6. soar

High-Frequency Words

7. ____________ 7. learn
8. ____________ 8. sure

Name ______________________________

A. Read the words in the box. Then sort the words.

born	core	corn	more	roar	soar

Words with ore	Words with oar	Words with or

B. Think of new words you can add to the chart.

Name ______________________________

A. Read the words in the box. Then sort the words.

born	core	corn	more	oar	roar

Words with ore	**Words with oar**	**Words with or**

B. Think of words that have the same spellings. Add them to the chart.

Name ______________________________

A. Read the words in the box. Then sort the words.

born	core	corn	more	pork	roar	soar	store

Words with ore	**Words with oar**	**Words with or**

B. Think of new words you can add to the chart.

Name ____________________

born	corn	core	more	roar
soar	her	dirt	learn	sure

Read the words in the box out loud. Then look at each set of words. One word in each set is spelled correctly. Use a pencil to fill in the circle in front of that word.

1. ○ dert
   ○ durt
   ○ dirt

2. ○ soer
   ○ soor
   ○ soar

3. ○ cor
   ○ core
   ○ cour

4. ○ sure
   ○ shur
   ○ sur

5. ○ hir
   ○ her
   ○ hur

6. ○ more
   ○ moor
   ○ mor

7. ○ ruar
   ○ roar
   ○ roer

8. ○ boarn
   ○ born
   ○ boern

Name ____________________

Trace and write <u>R</u> and <u>r.</u> Then copy the sentence. Make sure to leave spaces between words. Write neatly.

Rr

R R R R R

R R R

r r r r r r r

r r r

Rob and Ron read.

Name ______________________________

An **abbreviation** is a short way of writing a word. Most abbreviations end with a period.

Saturday ⟶ Sat.   September ⟶ Sept.

Write the abbreviation for each word. Remember to use a period.

1. August ____________
2. Road ____________
3. Monday ____________
4. February ____________
5. Thursday ____________
6. March ____________
7. November ____________
8. October ____________
9. Doctor ____________
10. January ____________

Name ______________________________

A. Read each sentence out loud. Then write the abbreviation for the underlined word in each sentence.

1. It snows in <u>December</u>. ____________

2. <u>Mister</u> Smith is my teacher. ____________

3. Pam lives on Main <u>Street</u>. ____________

4. Norm plants seeds in <u>April</u>. ____________

B. Use one of abbreviations your wrote above to write a new sentence.

____

____

Name ________________________________

Read and spell the words in the box. Complete each sentence with a word from the box. Read the sentences out loud.

began	better	guess	learn	right	sure

1. Mom ____________________ to cut the cake.

2. We will ____________________ how to plant a tree.

3. Can you ____________________ what is in the box?

4. I am ____________________ I will do well on my test.

5. I like this book ____________________ than that one.

6. This is the ____________________ way to ride a bike.

Name ______________________________

An **idea** is a picture you see in your head.
I have a good idea for a story.

Something that is **unusual** is not common.
What an unusual hat you have!

A. Write idea or unusual to complete each sentence.

1. Dan has an ____________________ for fixing the vase.

2. That is an ____________________ house.

B. Read the words in the box. Write your own sentence using one of the words.

leaped	stretched

____

Name ______________________________

A **prefix** is a word part added to the beginning of a word. A prefix changes the meaning of the word.

The prefix re- means "again": **re** + read = **reread**

Reread means "to read again."

The prefix un- means "not": **un + real** = **unreal**

Unreal means "not real."

A. Add the prefixes. Match the words to the pictures.

1. re + do = ______________________

2. un + pack = ______________________

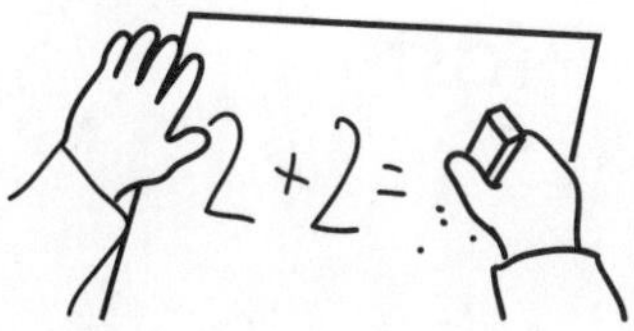

B. Add re- or un- to a word in the box to make a new word. Write a sentence with the new word.

happy	send

____

____

Name ______________________________

Add **-er** to an adjective to compare two people, places, or things.

Example: Flip's ears are **smaller** than Nell's ears.

Add **-est** to an adjective that compares three or more people, places, or things.

Example: Pip's ears are the **smallest** ears of all.

A. Write the adjectives that compare.

	add -er	add -est
1. fast	______________	______________
2. slow	______________	______________

B. Underline the adjective that compares.

1. Mike is the tallest boy in his class.

2. We had a longer recess today than yesterday.

Name ______________________________

A. Read the draft model. Find the errors.

Draft Model

The monkey was loudest than the bird.
Then the lion beegan to rore.
He was the louder of all!

B. Revise the draft. Make sure you use -er and -est for adjectives correctly. Fix any spelling errors.

____

____

____

____

____

Connect to Writing

C. Look in your writer's notebook. Make sure you used adjectives with -er and -est correctly.

Name ____

Add -<u>**er**</u> to most adjectives to compare two nouns.

Add -<u>**est**</u> to most adjectives to compare three or more nouns.

Days, months, and holidays are **proper nouns**. All **proper nouns** begin with a capital letter.

Circle the sentences that are written correctly.

1. My dog is biggest than your Dog.

   My dog is big than your dog.

   My dog is bigger than your dog.

2. I made the greatest catch ever on Saturday.

   I made the greater catch ever on saturday.

   I made the great catch ever on Saturday.

3. Flag day is in June.

   Flag day is in june.

   Flag Day is in June.

4. We were off from school on Martin luther king day.

   We were off from school on Martin Luther king day.

   We were off from school on Martin Luther King Day.

KK made some changes. The cuff worked much better than before. Soon lots of people wore her cuff. KK's idea was a hit!

Connect to Community: Have children talk to a family member about a great idea they've had for a new invention.

Good Ideas

Anyone can invent! Ben Franklin invented a stove and glasses. But even kids can invent. Here is one real story.

Teacher Directions: Have children establish a purpose for reading the take-home story.

KK liked winter. She liked to play outside. But her hands got so cold in the snow. She wanted to spend more time in the snow.

②

KK had a good idea. She made a fleece cuff. But it did not work too well. It still let snow in.

③

Name ____

Listen to the word your teacher says. Replace the sound. Circle the picture of the new word you made.

1.			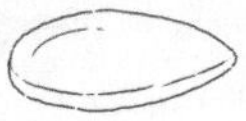
2.			
3.			
4.			
5.	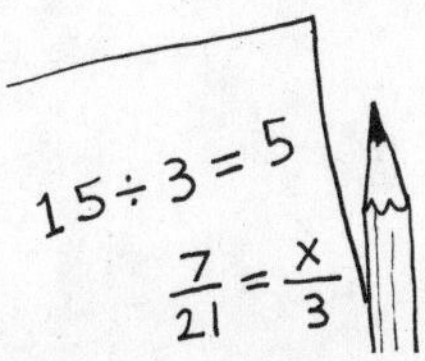	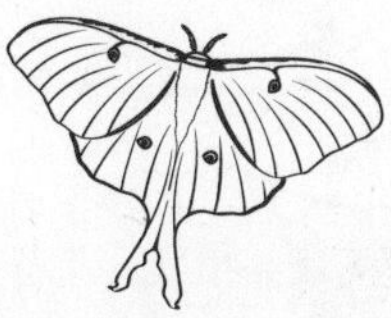	

Teacher Directions: I. Model: *This is the picture for the word* sad. *I can change the middle sound /a/ to /ē/ to make a new word. Listen to the new word:* seed. Circle the picture for the word *seed.* 2. Say *house.* Replace the /h/ sound with / m/. 3. Say *bed.* Replace the /e/ sound with /ûr/. 4. Say *cat.* Replace the /a/ sound with /är/. 5. Say *math.* Replace the /a/ sound with /ow/.

Name ______________________________

Say each picture name. Say the ending sounds. Circle the picture whose name has the same ending sound as the first picture in the row.

1.   

2. 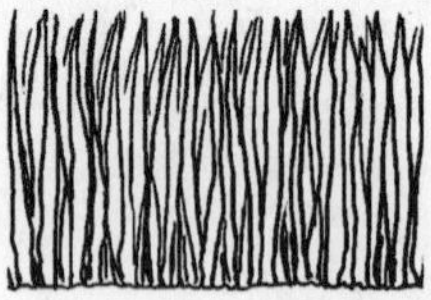  

3. 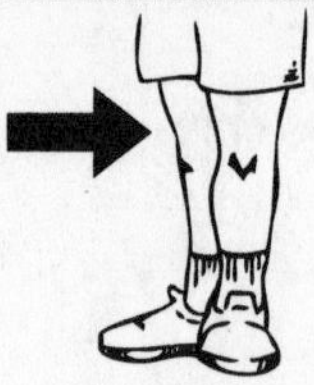  

4.   

5.   

Teacher Directions: Model item 1 by saying /k/ /ē/. Emphasize the ending sound. Then say *eel* and *bee* and explicitly compare ending sounds. Say: *The words* key *and* bee *have the same ending sound: /ē/.* Eel *has a different ending sound: /l/.* Guide children to circle the picture of the bee.

Name ______________________________

The letters <u>ou</u> and <u>ow</u> stand for the sound you hear in the middle of **m<u>ou</u>th** and **t<u>ow</u>n**.

Circle the picture whose name has the same sound you hear in the middle of <u>town</u>. Write <u>ou</u> or <u>ow</u> to complete the word that names the picture. Read the word.

1.    cr ________ n

2.    h ________ se

3. 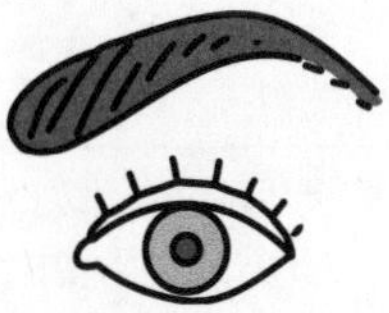   br ________

4.    m ________ se

Name ______________________________

A. Read the words in the box. Write the name of each picture. Then write a word from the box that rhymes with it.

mouse	frown	grouch	plow

1. 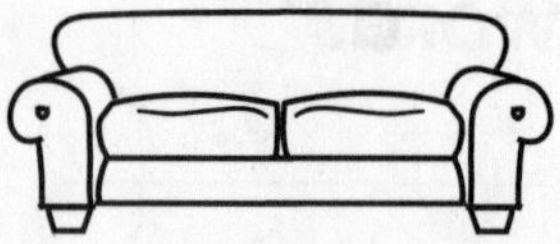 ______________ ______________

2.  ______________ ______________

3.  ______________ ______________

4.  ______________ ______________

B. Add one letter to make a new word with the same sound you hear in the middle of town.

1. pond ______________ **2.** shot ______________

Name ______________________________

Fold back the paper along the dotted line. Use the blanks to write each word as it is read aloud. When you finish the test, unfold the paper. Use the list at the right to correct any spelling mistakes.

1. ____________________ 1. cow
2. ____________________ 2. town
3. ____________________ 3. mouse
4. ____________________ 4. how
5. ____________________ 5. out
6. ____________________ 6. mouth

High-Frequency Words

7. ____________________ 7. nothing

8. ____________________ 8. early

Name ______________________________

A. Read the words in the box. Then sort the words.

cow	how	mouse	mouth	out	town

Words with ou	**Words with ow**

B. Think of new words you can add to the chart.

Name ______________________________

A. Read the words in the box. Then sort the words.

cow	how	out	sour	town	trout

Words with ou	Words with ow

B. Think of new words you can add to the chart.

Name ______________________________

A. Read the words in the box. Then sort the words.

brown cloud cow how mouse mouth out town

Words with ou	Words with ow

B. Think of new words to add to the chart.

Name ______________________

cow	town	mouse	how	out
mouth	born	roar	nothing	early

A. Read the words in the box. Change one letter in each word below to make a spelling word. Write the word.

1. down ______________
2. our ______________
3. south ______________
4. soar ______________
5. horn ______________
6. house ______________

B. Look at the words you wrote above. Circle the words that have the sound you hear at the end of how.

C. Write these spelling words in ABC order.

cow how roar nothing early town

Name ______________________

Trace and write X and x. Then copy the sentence. Make sure to leave spaces between words. Write neatly.

Xx

1 2

X X X X X X

X X X

1 2

x x x x x x x x

x x x

Max has six boxes.

Name ______________________________

Use the ending -er to compare two things:

I am a **fast** runner. Min is **faster** than I am.

Use the ending -est to compare three or more things:

Pam is the **fastest** runner of all.

Add the ending -er or -est to the word in parentheses to complete the sentence.

1. I am the ______________ girl in my family. (old)

2. My dad is ______________ than my mom. (short)

3. This box is ______________ than that one. (light)

4. Sam has the ______________ desk in the class. (neat)

5. The Sun is much ______________ than the Moon. (bright)

Name ______________________________

A. Circle the word that completes each sentence.

1. This is the (longer, longest) book I have read.

2. Kathy can read (faster, fastest) than me.

3. We both like Sam. She is the (smarter, smartest) character in the book.

B. Use one of the words you circled above to write a new sentence.

Name ______________________________

Read each sentence out loud. Match each sentence to a picture.

1. Her socks are not the same **color**.

a. 

2. There is **nothing** left to eat.

b. 

3. It is too **early** to wake up.

c. 

4. He **thought** it might rain.

d. 

5. **Oh**, no! The dog is digging up the garden!

e. 

6. I want this hat **instead**.

f. 

Name ______________________________

Write a sentence that uses each of the words below.

1. scrambled

2. suddenly

3. idea

4. unusual

Name ________________________________

A **suffix** is a word part added to the end of a word to make a new word.

The suffix -<u>or</u> means "a person who."
The suffix -<u>ful</u> means "full of."
The suffix -<u>less</u> means "without."
The suffix -<u>ly</u> means "in a way that is."

Read each sentence. Use the meaning of -<u>or</u>, -<u>ful</u>, -<u>less</u>, or -<u>ly</u> as a clue to the meaning of the bold word. Match the sentence with the word's meaning.

1. The new puppy is **playful**.	in a way that is bold
2. Dad is a good **sailor**.	a person who visits
3. The glass of water is **colorless**.	full of play
4. Please be **careful** on the slide.	a person who sails
5. The hero sang **boldly**.	without color
6. There is a **visitor** at the door.	full of care

Name ____________________

Use **a** with nouns that start with a consonant.

Use **an** with nouns that start with a vowel.

Use **this** for a noun that is close.

Use **that** for a noun that is far away.

A. Write a, an, this, or that to complete each sentence.

1. Vincent is ______ artist.

2. The cab is here. We will take ______ cab.

3. We can see ______ bird from far away.

B. Read the sentences. Find the errors. Write the sentences correctly.

4. I have a ant farm. Billy has an dog.

____

____

Name ________________________________

A. Read the draft model. Find the errors.

Draft Model

Amy wants an glass of milk. We are all owt of milk. She will have a apple insted.

B. Revise the draft. Make sure you use a and an correctly. Fix any spelling errors.

____

____

____

____

Connect to Writing

C. Look in your writer's notebook. Make sure you used a and an correctly.

Name ______________________________

A and **an** are adjectives that tell which one. Use **a** with nouns that start with a consonant. Use **an** with nouns that start with a vowel sound. Use **this** for a noun that is close. Use **that** for a noun that is far away.

All important words in book titles begin with capital letters. Underline book titles.

Write C if the sentence is correct. If the sentence is incorrect, write X and circle the mistakes.

1. We took an ride to a park. __________

2. This is a fun day. __________

3. My New Brother is a book about a baby. __________

4. We took that bus to school. __________

5. We read The Happy camper in class today. __________

They played some more.
Then Dad said, "You can look now. We are back at our brown house."
"That wasn't boring at all!" said Howie.

Connect to Community: Have children talk to a family member about things they like to do when they're bored.

Dad's Game

Howie and Dad have a long ride home.
"I do not like the bus ride," said Howie.
"It is so boring."

Teacher Directions: Have children establish a purpose for reading the take-home story.

"We can play a game," Dad said. "Don't look and guess where we are. I will give hints." Howie didn't look.

②

"I see swings and a slide," said Dad. "Where are we now?"
"It's the town park. Wow!" shouted Howie.

③

Name ______________________________

Listen to the sounds your teacher says. Blend the sounds together. Draw a picture of the word you made.

1.	**2.**
3.	**4.**

Teacher Directions: Model item 1 by saying /s/ /n/ /ō/. *Listen as I blend these sounds together: /snōōō/, snow.* Model drawing falling snow in the first box and have children copy. For items 2–4, have children listen to the sounds and blend them to form a word. 2. Say: /k/ /oy/ /n/; 3. Say: /c/ /l/ /ou/ /d/ /s/; 4. Say: /g/ /r/ /ā/ /p/ /s/.

Name ______________________________

Say the name of each picture. Count the sounds in each word. Then draw an X in one box for each sound.

1. 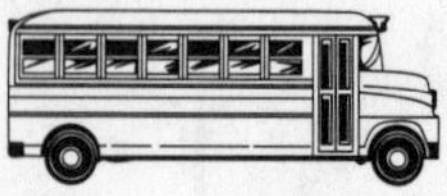					
2. 					
3. 					
4. 					
5. 					

Teacher Directions: Model item I by saying *bus.* Say: *I can say the sounds in the word* bus. *The word* bus *has three sounds: /b/ /u/ /s/. Say the sounds with me: /b/ /u/ /s/.*

Name ____

The letters **oi** and **oy** can stand for the sound you hear in the middle of **noise** and at the end of **joy**.

Read the words in the box. Use the words in the box to complete each sentence. Then read the sentences out loud.

enjoys	boil	Roy	toy	point	coin

1. This ______________________ is a dime.

2. My name is ______________________.

3. This is the baby's ______________________.

4. She ______________________ painting.

Name ______________________________

A. Write oi or oy to complete each word. Then write the word. Read the word you made out loud.

1.  b ______ l ______________

2.  p ______ n t ______________

3.  c o w b ______ ______________

4. 

c ______ n ______________

B. Add the letter y or i to make a new word with the sound you hear at the end of boy. Then write the word.

1. to ______________ 2. nose ______________

Name ______________________________

Fold back the paper along the dotted line. Use the blanks to write each word as it is read aloud. When you finish the test, unfold the paper. Use the list at the right to correct any spelling mistakes.

1. ____________ 1. spoil
2. ____________ 2. coin
3. ____________ 3. join
4. ____________ 4. joy
5. ____________ 5. toy
6. ____________ 6. boy

High-Frequency Words

7. ____________ 7. build
8. ____________ 8. fall

Name ______________________________

A. Read the words in the box. Then sort the words.

boy	coin	join	joy	spoil	toy

Words with oi	Words with oy

B. Think of new words you can add to the chart.

Name ______________________________

A. Read the words in the box. Then sort the words using the spellings.

boy	coin	join	joy	oil	toy

Words with oi	**Words with oy**

B. Think of words that have the same word endings. Add them to the chart.

Name ______________________________

A. Read the words in the box. Then sort the words.

boy coin enjoy join joy spoil toy voice

Words with oi	Words with oy

B. Think of new words to add to the chart.

Name ______________________________

A. Mark an X on the line next to the word that is spelled correctly.

1. coen ________	coyn ________	coin ________
2. billd ________	build ________	biuld ________
3. town ________	toun ________	tawn ________
4. joy ________	jooy ________	joi ________

B. In each row, put an X on the word that does not belong. Then write the spelling word.

5. head spoil broil ________________

6. house rope mouse ________________

7. late fall small ________________

Name ________________________________

Trace and write J and j. Then copy the sentence.
Make sure to leave spaces between words. Write neatly.

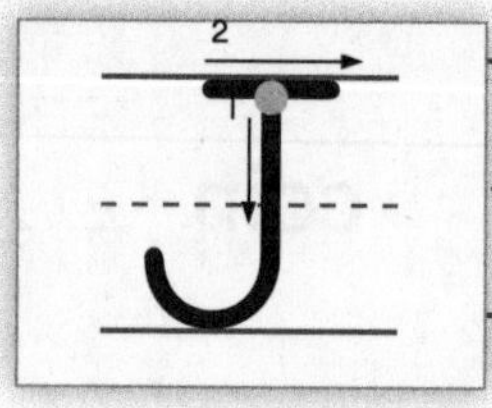

J J J J J

J J J

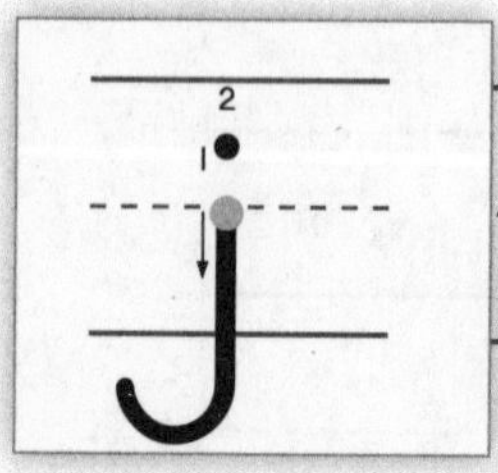

j j j j j j j j

j j j

Jan and Jim jump.

Name ______________________________

Many two-syllable words end with a **consonant + le**. The **consonant + le** always stay together in the last syllable.

tum/**ble** = tumble   sim/**ple** = simple

puz/**zle** = puzzle

Read the word. Draw a line between the syllables in each word. Write the two syllables.

1. title ____________ ____________
2. bubble ____________ ____________
3. handle ____________ ____________
4. crumble ____________ ____________
5. turtle ____________ ____________

Name ______________________________

A. Read each word out loud. Draw a line between the syllables in each word.

1. table
2. puddle
3. apple
4. marble
5. tumble
6. candle

B. Circle the word in each sentence that has a consonant + le syllable.

7. The turtle is very slow.

8. Becky thinks the test is simple.

9. Brad and I like to do puzzles.

C. Use one of the words from above to write a sentence.

Name ____________________

Read the words in the box out loud. Write the word that completes each sentence.

above	build	fall	knew	money	toward

1. The rain is going to ____________ !

2. We ____________ how to fix it.

3. They are walking ____________ the bus.

4. I save my ____________ in a bank.

5. They will ____________ something.

6. I see stars ____________ me.

Name ______________________________

balance: A thing can **balance** if it can stay in one place without falling.

section: A **section** is a small part of something bigger.

A. Write a word from the box to finish each sentence.

balance	section

1. That ________________ of the sky has too many stars to count!

2. Can Mike ________________ all those books?

B. Read the words in the box out loud. Write a new sentence using one of the words.

suddenly	scrambled

____

____

Name ____

An action word with the ending **-ed** means the action happened in the past.

An action word with the endings **-s** or **-ing** means the action is happening now.

If you see a new word, look for the ending **-ed** or **-ing** and a base word. Use the meanings of the word parts to figure out the meaning of the new word.

A. Underline the ending. Circle the base word. Then match the words to the pictures.

1. jumping

2. closed

3. walks

4. riding

Name ______________________________

A **preposition** comes before a noun or a pronoun. Together they make a prepositional phrase.

Some prepositions include **toward, in, of, on, above, for, during,** and **beyond**.

Examples: The picture is **on** the wall.

We will walk **toward** the park.

Complete the sentences with a preposition from the box.

for	during	off	beyond

1. We had a fire drill ______________ gym.

2. We jumped ______________ the step.

3. The field was built ______________ our team.

4. We went to the park way ______________ the soccer field.

Name ______________________________

A. Read the draft model. Find the errors.

Draft Model

Sam and I bring tois during the park.
We also play to the swings.

B. Revise the draft. Make sure you use the correct prepositions. Fix any errors you found.

Connect to Writing

C. Look in your writer's notebook. Make sure you used prepositions correctly.

Name ______________________________

Words such as **toward, in, of, on, above, for, during,** and **beyond** link nouns to other words in a sentence.

Name titles begin with capitals and end with periods.

Examples: **Mr.** Chen, **Mrs.** Mills, **Dr.** Don

Write C if the sentence is correct. If the sentence is incorrect, write X and circle the mistakes.

1. My dentist is dr. Mike. ________

2. I went there on Tuesday. ________

3. I got a cleaning beyond the visit. ________

4. Mrs. wall took me to the dentist. ________

5. It was mr. hopewell's turn after me. ________

Next, make a head. Use stones or coins to make a face. Stick in branches for arms. Give him a hat and a pointy nose. Enjoy!

Connect to Community: Teacher Directions: Have children talk to a family member about games they might play in the snow.

4

How to Build a Snowman

Look! Do you see wet, heavy snow fall from above? That means fun. You can build a snowman!

Teacher Directions: Have children establish a purpose for reading the take-home story.

1

First, roll some snow into a ball. It will get big and round. Next, roll a smaller snowball.

②

It is wet and heavy. What do you do next? Hoist it on top. Now, your snowman has a body.

③

Name ____________________

Listen to the sounds your teacher says. Blend the sounds together. Circle the picture that goes with the word.

1.

2.

3.

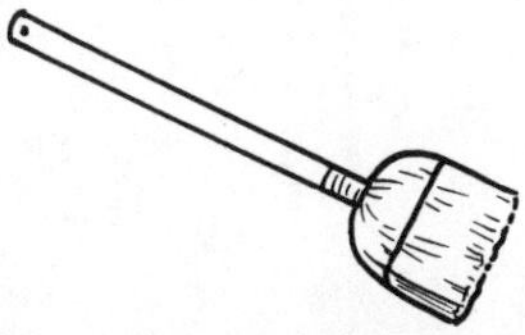

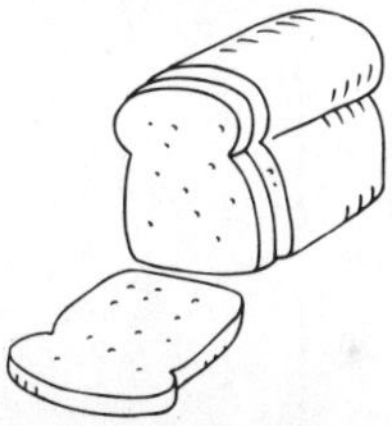

4.

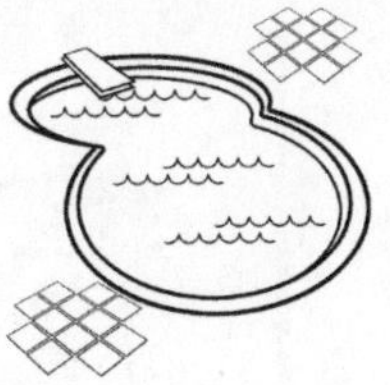

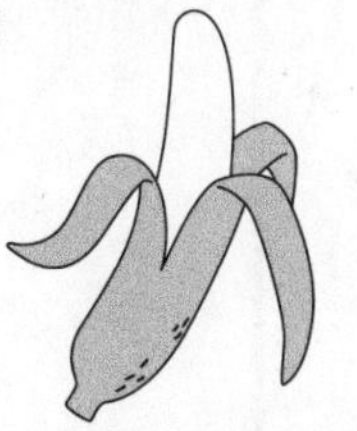

5.

Teacher Directions: Model item 1 by saying /k/ /ow/. *I will blend the sounds to make a word:* /kow/, *cow*. Guide children to circle the picture of the cow for item 1. For items 2–5, say the following sounds. Have students blend the sounds to say each word. Then have them circle the picture that shows it. 2. /k/ /oy/ /n/; 3. /b/ /r/ /ü/ /m/; 4. /p/ /ē/ /l/; 5. /t/ /ü/ /th/.

Name ______________________________________

Say the name of each picture. Count the sounds in each word. Then draw an X in one box for each sound.

1. 					
2. 					
3. 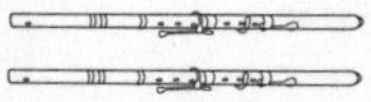					
4. 					
5. 					

Teacher Directions: Model item 1 by saying *ant*. Say: *I can say the sounds in the word* ant. *The word* ant *has three sounds: /a/ /n/ /t/. Say the sounds with me: /a/ /n/ /t/.*

Name ______________________________

The letters <u>oo</u> can stand for the sound you hear in the middle of **m<u>oo</u>n**.

The underlined letters in the words below show some other ways to spell the same sound.

tr<u>u</u>th **bl<u>ue</u>** **n<u>ew</u>** **t<u>u</u>b<u>e</u>** **fr<u>ui</u>t** **<u>you</u>**

Read the first word. Then circle another word in the row with the same ending sounds.

1.	**grew**	peg	goat	flew
2.	**spoon**	sock	noon	both
3.	**Ruth**	scarf	pail	truth
4.	**clue**	glue	call	nice
5.	**group**	game	soup	walk

Name ____________________

A. Read the word. Circle the letters that make the sound you hear at the end of <u>too</u>. Then circle the picture that the word names.

1. screw

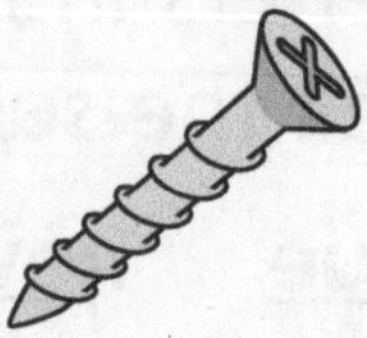

2. flute

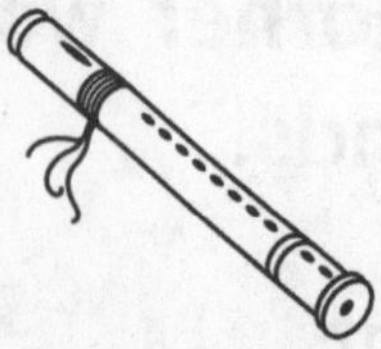

3. roof

4. fruit

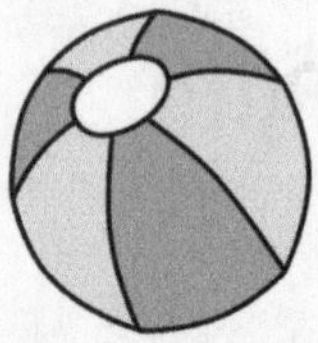

B. Add one letter to make a new word with the sound you hear in the middle of <u>June</u>. Then write the word.

1. tub ____________________

2. shot ____________________

Name ______________________________

Fold back the paper along the dotted line. Use the blanks to write each word as it is read aloud. When you finish the test, unfold the paper. Use the list at the right to correct any spelling mistakes.

1. ____________________ 1. moon
2. ____________________ 2. tune
3. ____________________ 3. flew
4. ____________________ 4. blue
5. ____________________ 5. fruit
6. ____________________ 6. soup

High-Frequency Words

7. ____________________ 7. enough
8. ____________________ 8. door

Name ______________________________

A. Read the words in the box. Then sort the words.

blue	flew	fruit	moon	soup	tune

Words with ew	Words with ui	Words with oo
______	______	______
______	______	______
______	______	______

Words with ou	Words with ue	Words with u_e
______	______	______
______	______	______
______	______	______

B. Think of new words to add to the chart.

Name ______________________________

A. Read the words in the box. Then sort the words.

blue	few	fruit	soup	too	tune

Words with ew	Words with ui	Words with oo

Words with ou	Words with ue	Words with u_e

B. Think of new words to add to the chart.

Name ______________________________

A. Read the words in the box. Then sort the words.

blue	chew	fruit	rude
flew	soup	spoon	truth

Words with ew	**Words with ui**	**Words with oo**
Words with ou	**Words with ue**	**Words with u_e**
Words with u		

B. Think of new words to add to the chart.

Name ____________________

moon	tune	flew	blue	fruit
soup	toy	coin	enough	door

A. Mark an X next to the word spelled correctly.

1. fleu ______ felew ______ flew ______

2. toone ______ tune ______ tuun ______

3. enuff ______ enough ______ enogh ______

4. blue ______ bleu ______ belu ______

B. Use a letter from the box to finish writing the words.

t	**n**	**d**	**c**

5. coi ______ 6. ______ oor

Name ______________________________

Trace and write <u>Q</u> and <u>q</u>. Then copy the sentence.
Make sure to leave spaces between words. Write neatly.

Q Q Q Q Q Q

Q Q Q

q q q q q q q q q

q q q

Quin is quite quick.

Name ________________________________

A **suffix** is a word part you can add to the end of a word to change its meaning.

The suffix **-ful** means **full** or **full of**.
The word **helpful** means **full of help**.

The suffix **-less** means **without**.
The word **helpless** means **without help**.

Circle the suffix in each word.

1. fearless
2. painless
3. useless
4. joyful
5. hopeful
6. useful
7. senseless
8. fearful
9. painful
10. pointless

Name ______________________________

A. Match the word to its meaning.

I. fearless	a. full of hope
2. hopeful	b. without pain
3. joyful	c. without fear
4. painless	d. full of joy

B. Use one of the words from above to write a new sentence.

Name ______________________________

Read and spell each word in the box. Complete each sentence. Use one of the words in the box.

answer	brought	busy	door	enough	eyes

1. Gram ____________ me a gift today.

2. We use our ____________ to see.

3. Dad said, "Please ____________ me now."

4. Mom is too ____________ to go to the park today.

5. Do we have ____________ eggs to make the cupcakes?

6. Please close the ____________ when you come in.

Name ______________________________

Read the words in the box out loud. Complete each sentence. Use a word from the box.

emergency	demand	balance	section

I. The coaches ______________ that their teams work hard.

2. We learned what to do in case of an ______________ .

3. I like this ______________ of the book.

4. The bike rider has good ______________ .

Name ______________________________

Synonyms are words with the same or almost the same meaning.

Some synonyms for **happy** are **glad** and **joyful**.

A. Circle the two words that have the same or almost the same meaning.

1.	sparkle	glow	funny
2.	none	cold	chilly
3.	busy	build	make
4.	angry	happy	mad
5.	shout	found	yell
6.	twirl	spin	grab

B. Write a sentence using a word you circled above.

____

____

Name ______________________________

Remember that a **noun** is a person, place, or thing.

A **pronoun** is a word that takes the place of a noun.

Ken is at school. **He** is at school.

The pronoun **he** takes the place of the noun **Ken**.

Some other pronouns are **she, we, it, they, you,** and **I**.

Circle the pronoun that takes the place of the underlined word or words in the sentence.

1. Dave likes to help others.	It	He
2. Missy shared her lunch with us.	She	They
3. Carl and Sari will have a bake sale.	I	They
4. I will take this book to my friend.	it	you
5. James can wash the car.	He	They

Name ____________________

A. Read the draft model. Circle spelling and capitalization errors.

Draft Model

Pam is bisy painting.

i will help.

Pam and I use bleu paint.

B. Now revise the draft by replacing the underlined nouns with pronouns. Make sure to capitalize the word I and use punctuation correctly. Make sure to correct the spelling of high-frequency words.

____

____

____

Connect to Writing

C. Look in your writer's notebook. Make sure you used pronouns correctly. Make sure to capitalize the word I and use punctuation correctly. Make sure to correct the spelling of high-frequency words.

Name ______________________________

The **pronoun I** is always a capital letter.

Examples: I help my Mom bake bread.
Mom says that I am a good helper.

A. Cross out I if it is not written correctly. Write the sentence correctly. Copy the sentence if it is correct.

1. i will be six in a few days.

____

2. Dad said that I could have a big party.

____

3. i think that Mom and i will make a big cake.

____

B. Replace the underlined words with a pronoun.

4. My pals will come to the party.

____

The pals drank cool water. Soon, the tree house was done. "I couldn't have done it without my new pals!" said Raccoon.

Connect to Community: Have children talk to a family member about a time their friends helped them.

④

Working Together

Raccoon was building a tree house. "This is the best tree house ever," he said. "But it's a lot of work. It is hard to do alone."

Teacher Directions: Have children establish a purpose for reading the take-home story.

①

Just then, Moose came by. "I can help you," he said. "I even have my tools. We can work together."

②

Next, Goose flew by. "What a great tree house!" she said. "I can help. I will get cool water for you to drink."

③

Name ______________________________

Look at each picture. Say the name of each picture out loud. Say the middle sounds. Circle the picture whose name has a different middle sound.

1.

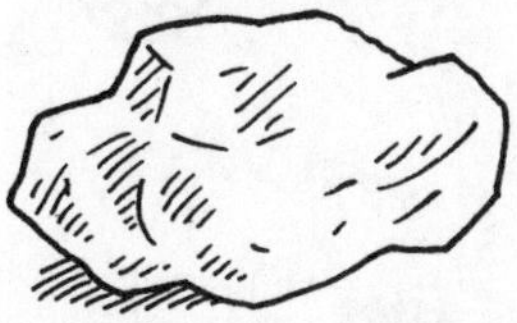

2.

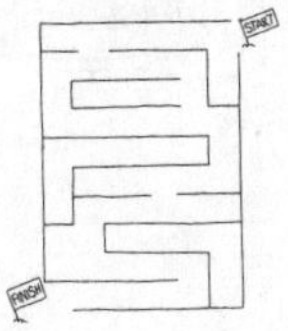
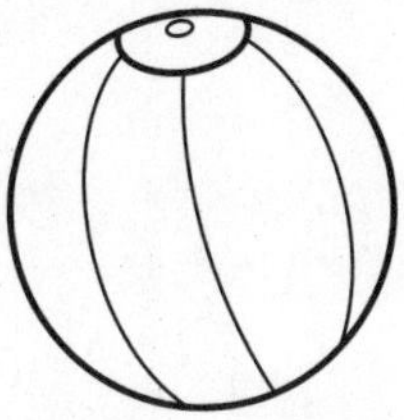

3.

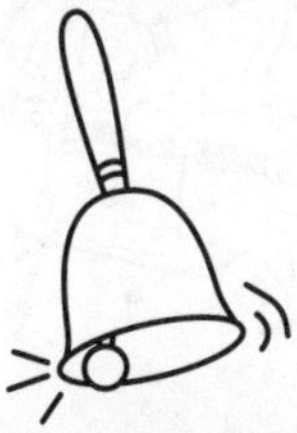

4.

5.

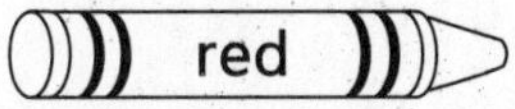

Teacher Directions: Model item 1 by saying *rock, fox,* and *sauce*. Repeat, stressing the difference between the /o/ and /ô/ vowel sounds. Say: *The words* rock *and* fox *have the same middle sound: /o/.* Sauce *has a different middle sound: /ô/.* Guide children to circle the picture of the sauce.

Name ______________________________________

Say the name of each picture below. Draw a line matching the pictures that have their first and last sounds reversed.

1.

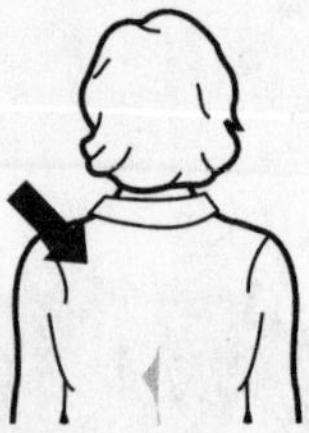

a.

2. **10**

b.

3.

c.

4.

d.

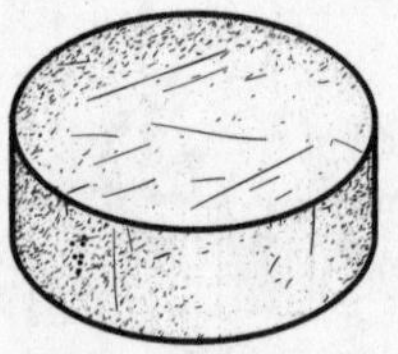

5.

e.

Teacher Directions: Model item 1 by saying back. Have children repeat the word. Explicitly say each phoneme: /b/ /a/ /k/. Say: *I'm going to reverse the first sound, /b/, and the last sound, /k/, in the word* back: /k/ /a/ /b/. Guide children to match back to cab.

Name ______________________________

Say **paw**. The same vowel sound can be spelled with **a** as in **mall**, **au** as in **fault**, **augh** as in **taught**, and **al** as in **talk**.

Write the words from the box that have the same sound-spelling as the name of the picture.

stalk	taught	fall	claw	cause

1. crawl ______________________

2. sauce ______________________

3. call ______________________

4. caught ______________________

5. walk ______________________

Name ______________________________

A. Use the letters a, aw, au, augh, or al to complete each word. Write the letters on the line.

1. cl ________

2. t ________ t

3. b ________ ll

4. c ________ t

B. Change one letter to make a new word with sound you hear in the middle of taught. Then write the word.

1. down ________ **3.** bill ________

2. hail ________ **4.** fell ________

Name ______________________

Fold back the paper along the dotted line. Use the blanks to write each word as it is read aloud. When you finish the test, unfold the paper. Use the list at the right to correct any spelling mistakes.

1. ____________	**1. haul**
2. ____________	**2. cause**
3. ____________	**3. saw**
4. ____________	**4. claw**
5. ____________	**5. paw**
6. ____________	**6. dawn**

High-Frequency Words

7. ____________	**7. love**
8. ____________	**8. friend**

Name ______________________________

A. Read the words in the box. Then sort the words.

cause	claw	dawn	haul	paw	saw

Words with <u>aw</u>	Words with <u>au</u>

B. Think of new words to add to the chart.

Name ______________________________

A. Read the words in the box. Then sort the words.

cause claw haul jaw paw saw

Words with aw	Words with au
______	______
______	______
______	______
______	______
______	______
______	______

B. Think of new words to add to the chart.

Name ______________________________

A. Read the words in the box. Then sort the words.

awful	cause	claw	dawn
fault	haul	paw	saw

Words with aw	Words with au

B. Think of new words to add to the chart.

Name ______________________________

haul	cause	saw	claw	paw
dawn	moon	soup	love	friend

Read the words in the box out loud. Look at each set of words. One word in each set is spelled correctly. Fill in the circle in front of that word.

1. ○ sawe
   ○ sau
   ○ saw

2. ○ soup
   ○ soop
   ○ sewp

3. ○ lov
   ○ love
   ○ luve

4. ○ doun
   ○ daun
   ○ dawn

5. ○ cawse
   ○ cause
   ○ cose

6. ○ paw
   ○ pau
   ○ pawe

7. ○ houl
   ○ hawl
   ○ haul

8. ○ clauw
   ○ claw
   ○ claugh

Name ____________________

Read the first two lines of the story. Look at the picture. Then write the end of the story. Make sure you leave spaces between words. Write neatly.

Tom likes to camp.

He set up his tent.

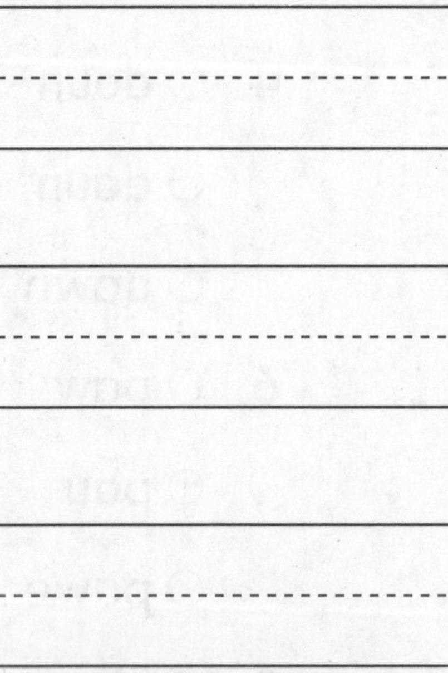

Name ____________________

Vowel teams are formed by two letters in a word that stand for one vowel sound. The underlined letters in these words are examples of vowel teams.

heat **hood** **stay** **out** **boy** **saw**

Vowel teams stay together in the same syllable.

oat/meal **row/ing**

Underline the vowel teams in each word. Draw a line between the syllables.

1. playground
2. neatest
3. drawing
4. mailbox
5. peeling
6. growing
7. raincoat
8. cowboy
9. bookcase
10. sixteen

Name ______________________________

A. Circle the words with a vowel teams in each sentence. Underline the vowel team in the words you circle. Draw a line between the syllables.

1. Bill and Kim will go outside.

2. Mom will reread the story to us.

3. Maybe I will need my raincoat today.

4. Dad made us oatmeal.

B. Use one of the words you circled above to write a new sentence.

____

____

Name ______________________________

A. Read the words in the box out loud. Complete each sentence. Use one of the words in the box.

brother	father	friend	love	mother	picture

1. My ____________ Liz goes to my school.

2. I smiled for my class ____________.

3. I ____________ to run around the park.

4. My ____________ and ____________ tell me to go to bed.

5. Paul's ____________ is my friend.

Name ______________________________

When you **accept** something, you take it or agree to it.
If you do something **often**, you do it a lot.

A. Use a word from the box to finish each sentence.

accept   often

1. Chris visits the park __________ to ride his bike.

2. Kyle was ready to __________ the award from the mayor.

B. Read the words. Write your own sentence using a word from the box.

demand   emergency

____

Name ______________________________

Words with opposite meanings are called **antonyms.**

Read each sentence. Circle the word that has the <u>opposite</u> meaning of the bold word.

1. The **tiny** mouse ran away.

small | cute | huge

2. Paul **always** plays baseball on Fridays.

faster | often | never

3. Melissa told us the show was **great**.

long | awful | good

4. The ride was very **loud**.

wild | noisy | quiet

5. Jimmy felt **better** after a day in bed.

worse | happy | best

6. Dad can climb the **tall** ladder.

short | safe | big

Name ____

A **pronoun** is a word that takes the place of a noun.

A **possessive** pronoun shows who or what has or owns something.

This is Max's toy. This is his toy.

The possessive pronouns **my, your, his, her, its, our,** and **their** are used before nouns.

my hat	your coat	his book	her cat
its place	our home	their car	

Circle the possessive pronoun that belongs in the sentence.

1. Jane broke (her, their) new glasses.

2. The red bird had yellow tips on (my, its) wings.

3. My brother and I walked to (our, its) house.

4. Miss Lee asked me, "Is this (its, your) book?"

5. Mom and Dad liked (their, its) gifts.

6. The dog lost (its, their) bone.

Name ______________________________

A. Read the draft model. Circle the spelling errors.

Draft Model

Lily saw a little faun.

She drew a piktur of the fawn's face.
Paul liked Lily's drawing.

B. Now revise the draft by replacing the underlined words with a possessive pronoun. Fix any spelling errors you found. Rewrite the sentences below.

____

____

____

____

Connect to Writing

C. Look in your writer's notebook. Make sure you used possessive pronouns correctly.

Name ______________________________

The **days of the week, months,** and **holidays** always begin with a capital letter.

Examples: We will help clean the park on **Sunday, April** 22nd for **Earth Day!**

Circle the sentence that is correct.

1. Each saturday Jill goes to swim class.

Each Saturday Jill goes to swim class.

2. My dad and I saw a parade on Labor Day.

My dad and I saw a parade on labor day.

3. Is your birthday on Monday or tuesday?

Is your birthday on Monday or Tuesday?

4. I think that June is the best month for outdoor fun.

I think that june is the best month for outdoor fun.

5. We will go camping at the lake in may.

We will go camping at the lake in May.

Coaches

Coaches help us learn to play a sport. First, they teach the rules of the sport. That way the players know the game.

Teacher Directions: Have children establish a purpose for reading the take-home story.

Coaches love to play, teach, and talk about their sport. They help us love it, too!

Connect to Community: Have children talk to a family member about a sport they like.

Coaches help players in lots of ways. They show players how to throw and hit the ball. They train players to run fast.

②

Coaches also help the players work together. They teach players to all get along and to help each other. That's because this helps make a good team.

③

Name ______________________________

Look at each picture. Say the name of each picture out loud. Say the beginning sounds. Circle the picture whose name has a different beginning sound.

1.

2.

3.

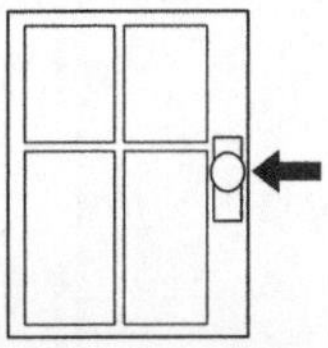

4.

5.

Teacher Directions: Model item 1 by saying *wrap, ran,* and *walk*. Repeat, stressing the difference between the /r/ and /hw/ beginning sounds. Say: *The words* wrap *and* ran *have the same beginning sound: /r/.* Walk *has a different beginning sound: /hw/.* Guide children to circle the picture of the girls walking.

Name ______________________________

Say the name of each picture. Count the sounds in each word. Then draw an X in one box for each sound.

1. 					
2. 					
3. 					
4. 					
5. 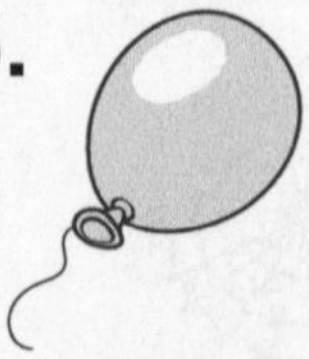					

Teacher Directions: Model item 1 by saying *store*. Say: *I can say the sounds in the word* store. *The word* store *has three sounds: /s/ /t/ /ôr/. Say the sounds with me: /s/ /t/ /ôr/.*

Name ______________________________

When you see **wr**, **kn**, **gn** at the beginning of a word or syllable, the first letter is silent.

wrap **kn**it **gn**aw

Circle the word that names each picture. Read the word out loud.

1.

knot not

2.

right write

3.

rats gnats

4.

need knead

5.

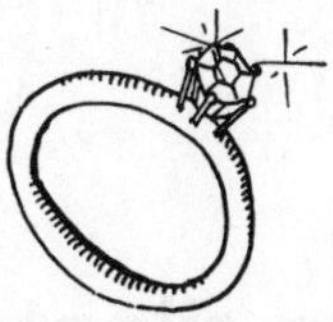

ring wring

6.

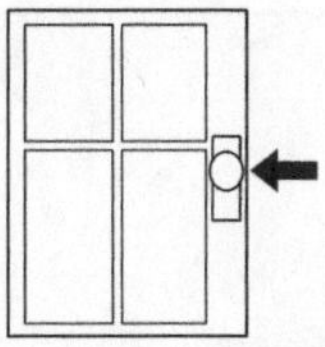

not knob

Name ______________________________

A. Read the words in the box. Write the word from the box that completes each sentence.

gnats	wring	kneel	knew	wrap

1. Mom likes to ______________ presents.

2. Nate does not like the ______________.

3. Dad ______________ I wanted new shoes.

4. I will ______________ the wet sheets.

B. Add one letter to make a new word with a silent letter. Then write the word.

1. not ______________ 2. ring ______________

Name ______________________

Fold back the paper along the dotted line. Use the blanks to write each word as it is read aloud. When you finish the test, unfold the paper. Use the list at the right to correct any spelling mistakes.

1. ______________	**1. gnat**
2. ______________	**2. gnu**
3. ______________	**3. know**
4. ______________	**4. knife**
5. ______________	**5. write**
6. ______________	**6. wrong**
7. ______________	**7. been**
8. ______________	**8. their**

High-Frequency Words

Name ____________________

A. Read the words in the box. Then sort the words.

gnat	knife	write	gnu	know	wrong

Words with kn	Words with gn	Words with wr

B. Think of new words to add to the chart.

Name ____________________

A. Read the words in the box. Then sort the words using the beginning of each word.

gnat	knot	write	knit	know	wrong

Words with kn	Words with gn	Words with wr

B. Think of words that start with silent letters. Add them to the chart.

Name ______________________________

A. Read the words in the box. Then sort the words.

gnat kneel write gnu wrong knife written know

Words with kn	Words with gn	Words with wr

B. Think of new words to add to the chart.

Name ______________________________

gnat	gnu	know	knife	write
wrong	cause	dawn	been	their

A. Use the letters in the box to finish writing a spelling word. Circle the picture that matches the word.

wr   kn   gn   aw

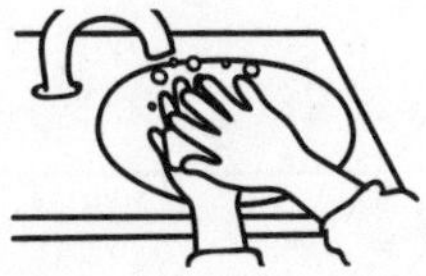
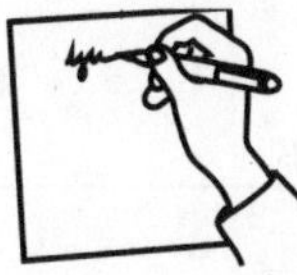

1. ______________ ite

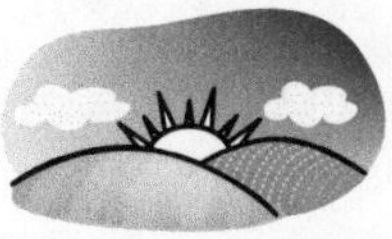

2. ______________ at

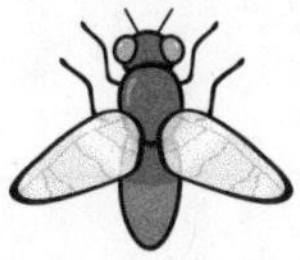
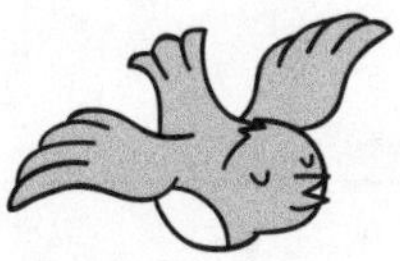

3. d ______________ n

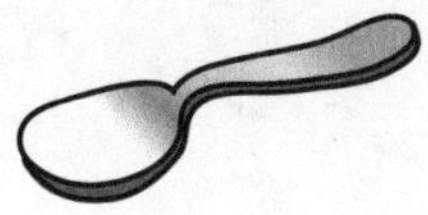

4. ______________ ife

B. Circle the spelling word that is correct.

5. thair   their   thier

6. rwong   rong   wrong

Name ______________________________

Read the first two lines of the story. Look at the picture. Then write the end of the story on the lines. Make sure you leave spaces between words. Write neatly.

Charlie likes mud.

Now he's dirty!

Name ______________________________

A **compound word** is a word made up of two smaller words. Read the two words. Then read the compound word.

ant + hill = anthill

Read each compound word. Read the two smaller words you see in each word. Write the two smaller words.

1. afternoon ____________ ____________

2. rowboat ____________ ____________

3. raindrop ____________ ____________

4. outside ____________ ____________

Name ______________________________

A. Circle the compound word in each sentence. Read each of the smaller words you see in the compound word. Then write the two smaller words.

1. Mom and I made a birdhouse out of wood.

_______________ _______________

2. We hung it in the backyard for the birds.

_______________ _______________

3. It looks so pretty in the sunlight.

_______________ _______________

B. Write your own sentence using one of the words you circled above.

____

____

Name ____________________

Read the words in the box out loud. Complete each sentence. Use the words from the word box.

been	children	month	question	their	year

1. We have ____________ playing all day.

2. June is the name of a ____________.

3. Raise your hand if you want to ask a ____________.

4. The ____________ are making a fort.

5. All the kids have ____________ books.

6. Last ____________, we were in kindergarten.

Name ________________________________

A **country** is a land where a group of people live.

We live in a country called the United States.

When a person **gathers** things, the things are put in the same place.

Sam gathers the mugs.

A. Write country or gathers to complete each sentence.

1. Spain is a ____________________.

2. Mr. Jones ____________________ our papers.

B. Write your own sentence using one of the words from the box.

accept	often

____

____

Name ______________________________

Writers can use **similes** to help readers picture details. A simile compares one thing to another using the words like or as.

Examples: The puddle is as big as a lake.

The wind felt like an ice cube.

A. Read each sentence. Underline the words like or as. Circle the two things that are compared.

1. The storm was like a roller coaster.

2. Paul's list is as long as a book.

3. The flashlight is like the Sun.

4. The blanket is as warm as a bath.

5. The house is as dark as a cave.

B. Write your own sentence using the words like or as.

____

Name ______________________________

Some **special pronouns,** such as **anyone, everyone, anything, everything, nothing, nobody, somebody,** and **anybody** do not name a special thing.

anyone means "any person"
everyone means "all people"
anything means "no special thing"
everything means "all things"
nothing means "no thing"
nobody means "no person"
somebody means "no special person"
anybody means "any person"

Circle the special pronoun in each sentence.

1. Meg spoke to everyone at the party.
2. Is there anything in your glass?
3. I spilled everything in the box when I fell.
4. Ana found nothing under the bed when she looked for her socks.
5. Do you know anyone who can help us rake leaves?
6. I didn't know anybody in that play.

Name ______________________________

A. Read the draft model. Circle the spelling errors.

Draft Model

Jill didn't now <u>the children</u> at the park.

<u>One of the kids</u> asked her to play.

Then she met <u>all the childrin</u> in the park.

B. Now revise the draft by replacing the underlined words with a special pronoun. Fix the errors you found. Rewrite the sentences below.

____

____

____

____

____

Connect to Writing

C. Look in your writer's notebook. Make sure you used special pronouns correctly.

Name ______________________________

Use **commas** to separate the date and year when writing a date.

Use **commas** after the greeting and closing in a letter.

Examples: June 6, 2020

Dear Ned,

I hope you like your new school. The kids in Miss Chan's class say, "Hi." We all miss you!

Your friend,
Jess

Read the letters. Add the missing commas.

1. October 2 2020

Dear Gram

I had so much fun on our trip to see the fall leaves. I hope we can go again next year! Thank you for taking me!

Your grandson
Ben

2. June 24 2020

Dear Kate

Thank you for asking me to your birthday party. I can't make it that day. I will be with my grandmother in Peach City all weekend.

Your pal
Ben

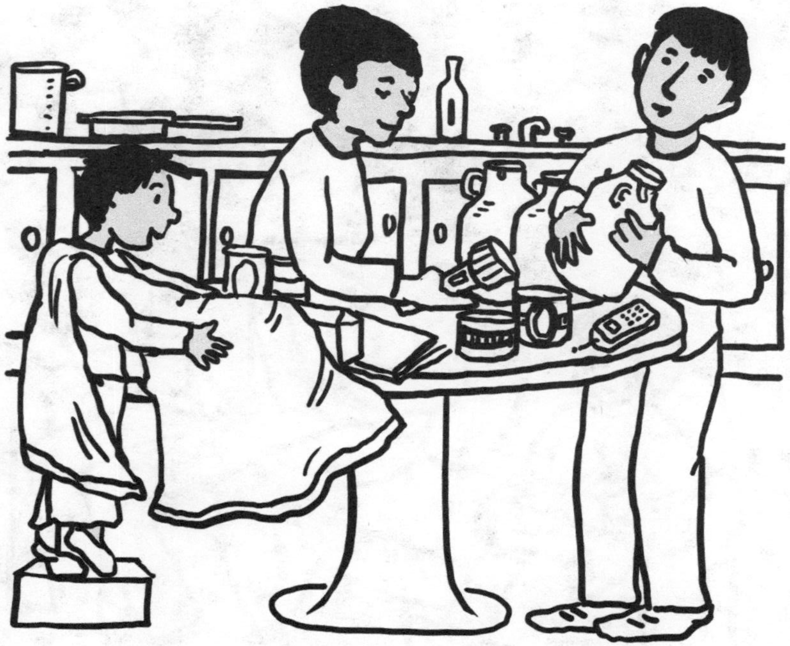

Paul wanted his blanket. He said, "We will need to stay warm." Dad got a phone. "We will be ready," said Dad.

Connect to Community: Have children talk to a family member about a time the weather affected them.

Storm Watch

"A big storm is coming," Mom said. "We need to get ready." Paul was worried. He did not like storms. They can wreck things.

Teacher Directions: Have children establish a purpose for reading the take-home story.

"There is time to plan," said Dad. "We have to find all the things we may need. We will need to stay inside."

2

"I will write a list," said Paul. Paul wrote the word "flashlight." "We will need light," said Paul. "In a storm, power can go out."

3

Name ______________________________

Listen to each word your teacher says. Add one syllable. Circle the picture for the new word you made.

1.

2.

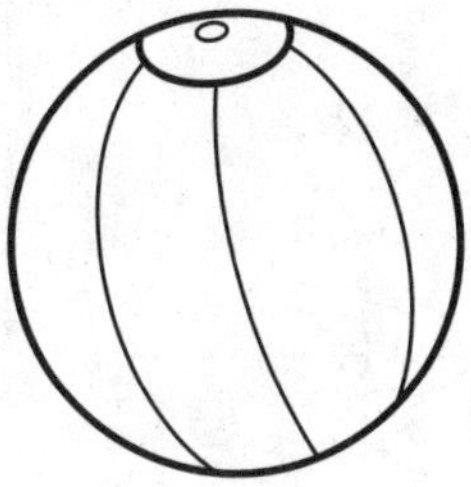

3.

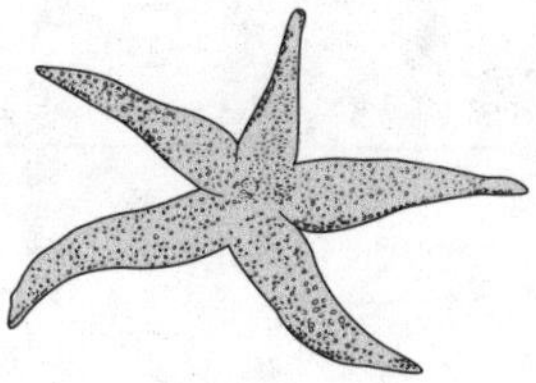

4.

Teacher Directions: 1. Model: *I can add a syllable to a word to make a new word. Listen to the word:* pop. *I can add the syllable corn to the ending of* pop *to make the new word:* popcorn. *Say the new word with me:* popcorn. 2. Say: *Add* el *to the beginning of* bow. 3. Say: *Add* fish *to the end of* star. 4. Say: *Add* note *to the beginning of* book.

Name ____

Say the name of each picture. Count the sounds in each word. Then draw an X in one box for each sound.

1. 					
2. 					
3. 					
4. 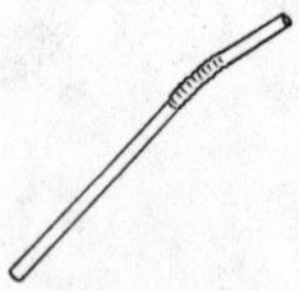					
5. 					

Teacher Directions: Model item 1 by saying *glue*. Say: *I can say the sounds in the word* glue. *The word* glue *has three sounds: /g/ /l/ /ü/. Say the sounds with me: /g/ /l/ /ü/.*

Name ______________________________

Sometimes three consonants form a **blend**.

scrap **splash** **spray** **street** **three** **shrub**

Read the first word. Then circle another word in the line with the same three-letter blend.

1. **street**	straw	tree	sharp
2. **shrub**	shred	should	both
3. **three**	thing	threw	tree
4. **scrap**	cry	scratch	school
5. **spray**	spot	soap	spring
6. **splash**	seat	play	split

Name ______________________________

A. Write the word on the line. Draw a line from the word to the picture it names.

I. thr + ee = ____________

a. 

2. scr + atch = ____________

b. 

3. spr + ay = ____________

c. 

4. spl + it = ____________

d. 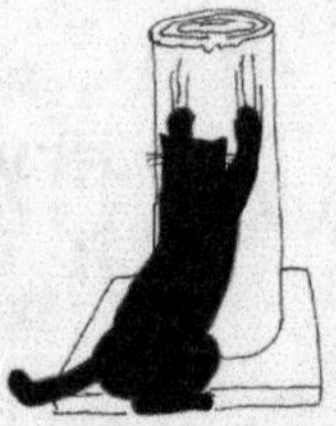

B. Add one letter to make a new word with a three-letter blend. Then write the word.

I. sting ____________ 2. stand ____________

Name ______________________

Fold back the paper along the dotted line. Use the blanks to write each word as it is read aloud. When you finish the test, unfold the paper. Use the list at the right to correct any spelling mistakes.

1. ______	**1. strike**
2. ______	**2. spray**
3. ______	**3. splash**
4. ______	**4. split**
5. ______	**5. scrape**
6. ______	**6. three**
High-Frequency Words 7. ______	**7. your**
8. ______	**8. heard**

Name ______________________________

A. Read the words in the box. Then sort the words.

scrape	splash	strike	split	three	spray

Words with spl	Words with str	Words with thr
____________	____________	____________
____________	____________	____________

Words with spr	Words with scr
____________	____________
____________	____________

B. Think of new words to add to the chart.

Name ____________________

A. Read the words in the box. Then sort the words.

scrap	splash	strike	scrub	three	split

Words with <u>spl</u>	Words with <u>str</u>
____________________	____________________
____________________	____________________

Words with <u>thr</u>	Words with <u>scr</u>
____________________	____________________
____________________	____________________

B. Think of new words to add to the chart.

____

Name ____________________

A. Read the words in the box. Then sort the words.

shrill	splash	scrape	spray
split	strike	three	string

Words with <u>spl</u>	Words with <u>str</u>	Words with <u>thr</u>
________	________	________
________	________	________
________	________	________
Words with <u>spr</u>	**Words with <u>scr</u>**	**Words with <u>shr</u>**
________	________	________

B. Think of new words to add to the chart.

Name ______________________________

strike	spray	splash	split	scrape
three	know	write	your	heard

A. Circle the word in each row that is spelled correctly.

1. rwite	wirt	write
2. yer	your	yur
3. heard	haerd	herad

B. Write the spelling word from the box at the top of the page that starts with the three-letter blend shown.

4. scr ______________________ 5. str ______________________

6. thr ______________________ 7. spr ______________________

8. spl ______________________ 9. spl ______________________

Name ____________________

A. Read the sentence and write it on the line. Make sure you use commas correctly. Write neatly.

It is May 11, 2021.

B. Read the sentence and write it on the line. Make sure to use colons correctly.

It is 2:15.

Name ______________________________

Add -ed to an action word to tell what happened in the past.
Add -ing to tell what is happening now.
Change some words before adding -ed or -ing.

race – e + ed = raced   try – y + i + ed = tried

drop + p + ing = dropping

Complete each sentence. Add -ed or -ing to the word in parentheses. Write the new word. Read the sentence.

1. I ______________ the dog after his bath. (dry)

2. My cat ______________ me yesterday. (scratch)

3. The bus ______________ here last week. (stop)

4. Mom is ______________ on the phone. (talk)

Name ______________________________

A. Circle the word that completes each sentence. Then read each sentence out loud.

1. Bruce (tried, trying) to finish his painting quickly.

2. It is (dried, drying) outside now.

3. He is (scrubbed, scrubbing) his paint brushes.

4. Jenny (raced, racing) to the finish line.

5. The bunny is (hopping, hopped) in the grass.

B. Use one of the words you circled above to write a new sentence.

____

____

____

____

Name ______________________

Read and spell the words in the box out loud. Complete each sentence. Use one of the words in the box.

before	front	heard	push	tomorrow	your

1. I helped Mom paint the ______________ door.

2. Is this ______________ book or mine?

3. Let's wash up ______________ we eat lunch.

4. We ______________ the thunder.

5. Will you ______________ me on the swing?

6. I have art class today and soccer ______________.

Name ______________________________

difficult: Something that is **difficult** is not easy.

nobody: **Nobody** means "no person."

A. Complete the sentences with words from the box.

difficult   nobody

1. Riding a bike can be ______________ for some and easy for others.

2. I heard a knock at the door, but ______________ was there.

B. Write your own sentence using one of the words below.

country   gathers

____

____

Name ______________________________

A **compound word** is a longer word made up of two smaller words. The word **birdhouse** is a compound word. Read each of the smaller words. Then read the compound word.

bird + house = birdhouse

A **birdhouse** is a house for birds to live in.

A. Draw a line between the two smaller words in each compound word. Use the two words to help you match the compound word to its meaning.

1. toolbox	a bag to carry books
2. snowball	a box to carry tools
3. toothbrush	a ball made of snow
4. bookbag	a brush to clean teeth

B. Write a sentence using a compound word above.

____

Name ______________________________

Use the pronouns **I, he, she, we,** and **they** in the subject of a sentence.

I read a book about kites.

Use the pronouns **me, him, her, us,** and **them** in the predicate of a sentence.

Dad gave me the book.

A. Circle the word that completes the sentence.

1. (I, Me) like to fly kites.

2. My dad likes to fly (they, them), too.

3. Mom and I will make (he, him) a kite.

4. (She, Her) will help (I, me) make the kite frame.

B. Read the draft model. Revise the draft by fixing errors you find. Rewrite it below.

5. Him thanks we for the kite!

____

____

Name ______________________________

A. Read the draft model. Find the errors.

Draft Model

Me want to plant seeds.
I dig holes in the frunt yard.
Soon, them will srpout!

B. Now revise the draft. Make sure you use pronouns correctly. Fix any spelling errors.

____

____

____

Connect to Writing

C. Look in your writer's notebook. Make sure you used pronouns correctly.

Name ______________________________

Remember to use **commas** to separate the date and year when writing a date.

Examples: I will be six on May 9, 2020.

Also use **commas** after the greeting and closing in a letter.

Examples: Dear Seth,

I hope you feel better soon.
We miss you at school.

Your friend,
Jess

Read the letters. Add the missing commas.

1. June 11 2020
Dear Grandfather

Thank you for helping me plant the peach tree in our backyard. One day we will pick some good peaches!

Your grandson
Chris

2. March 14 2020
Dear Milly

My class is putting on a play about making friends.

The play will be on March 25 2020.

I hope you can come and see me in the show.

Your friend
Jen

"We will start with strawberry cake," said Aunt Jane. "Then we will have pasta." Sue smiled. This would be a good birthday!

Connect to Community: Have children talk to family members about what they like to do on their birthdays.

4

Sue's Surprise

It was Sue's b… …her
mom and da…
was stayin…
She felt…
hopes s…

Teacher Direc…
take-home st…

2
The …
fun. But w…
do with Aunt J…

Sue always had a birthday
picnic with Mom and Dad.
three of them had
what would she
Jane?

"Time for our Silly
Supper," said Aunt Jane.
"On birthdays, I like to
eat out of order."

③

Name ______________________________

Say the name of each picture below. Draw a line matching the pictures that have their first and last sounds reversed.

1. 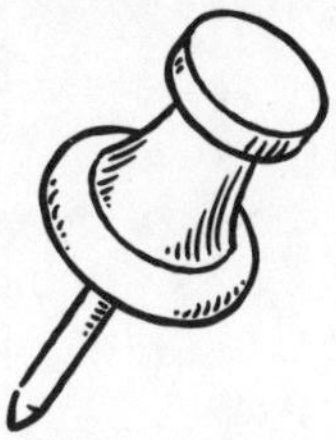

a. 

2. 

b. 

3. 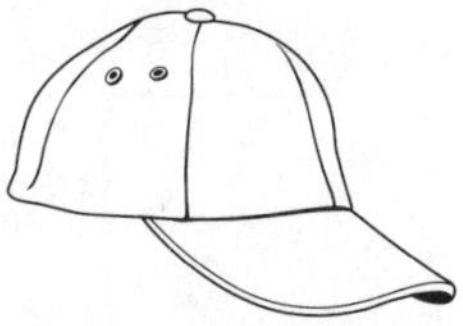

c. 

4. 

d. 

5. 

e. 

Teacher Directions: Model item 1 by saying *tack*. Have children repeat the word. Explicitly say each phoneme: /t/ /a/ /k/. Say: *I'm going to reverse the first sound, /t/, and the last sound, /k/, in the word* tack: */k/ /a/ /t/.* Guide children to match *tack* to *cat*.

Name ________________________________

Listen to the sounds your teacher says. Blend the sounds together. Draw a picture of the word you made.

1.	**2.**
3.	**4.**

Teacher Directions: Model item 1 by saying: */ch/ /âr/. Listen as I blend these sounds: /chââârrr/, chair.* Model drawing a chair in the first box and have children copy. For items 2–4, have children listen to the sounds and blend them to form a word. 2. Say: /ch/ /âr/; 3. Say: /h/ /âr/ /ē/; 4. Say: /s/ /t/ /âr/ /w/ /ā/.

Name ______________________________

The letters <u>air</u> together can make the sound you hear at the end of **ch<u>air</u>**.

The letters <u>are</u> and <u>ear</u> can also make the same sound, as in **sh<u>are</u>** and **p<u>ear</u>**.

Circle the word that completes the sentence. Then write the word.

1. Ruth has long ____________.

   heat   hair

2. My room is at the top of the ____________.

   stairs   stars

3. The noise might ____________ you.

   scarf   scare

4. I think I will ____________ a big coat today.

   wrote   wear

Name ______________________________

A. Read the word. Circle the letters that make the sound you hear at the end of ch<u>air</u>. Circle the picture that the word names.

1. square

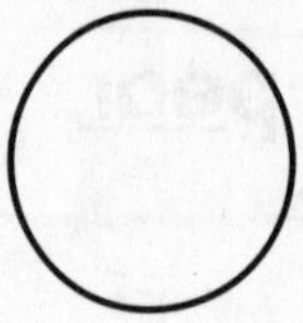

2. hair

3. pear

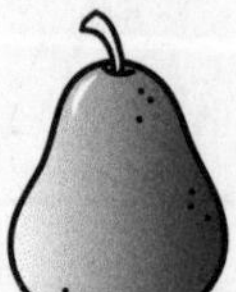

4. bear

B. Add one letter to make a new word with the sound you hear at the end of <u>pear</u>. Then write the word.

1. far ______________ 2. star ______________

Name ____________________

Fold back the paper along the dotted line. Use the blanks to write each word as it is read aloud. When you finish the test, unfold the paper. Use the list at the right to correct any spelling mistakes.

1. ____________	1. fair
2. ____________	2. pair
3. ____________	3. bear
4. ____________	4. wear
5. ____________	5. spare
6. ____________	6. share
High-Frequency Words 7. ____________	7. favorite
8. ____________	8. surprise

Name ____________________

A. Read the words in the box. Then sort the words.

bear	fair	share	wear	pair	spare

Words with air	Words with ear	Words with are

B. Think of new words to add to the chart.

____

Name ____

A. Read the words in the box. Then sort the words.

bear	fair	rare	wear	share	pair

Words with <u>air</u>	Words with <u>ear</u>	Words with <u>are</u>

B. Think of new words to add to the chart.

Name ______________________________

A. Read the words in the box. Then sort the words.

bear	fair	scare	spare
wear	careful	pair	share

Words with <u>air</u>	Words with <u>ear</u>	Words with <u>are</u>

B. Think of new words to add to the chart.

____

Name ____________________

fair	pair	bear	wear	spare
share	three	splash	favorite	surprise

Read the clue. Write the spelling word in the puzzle. Put one letter in each box.

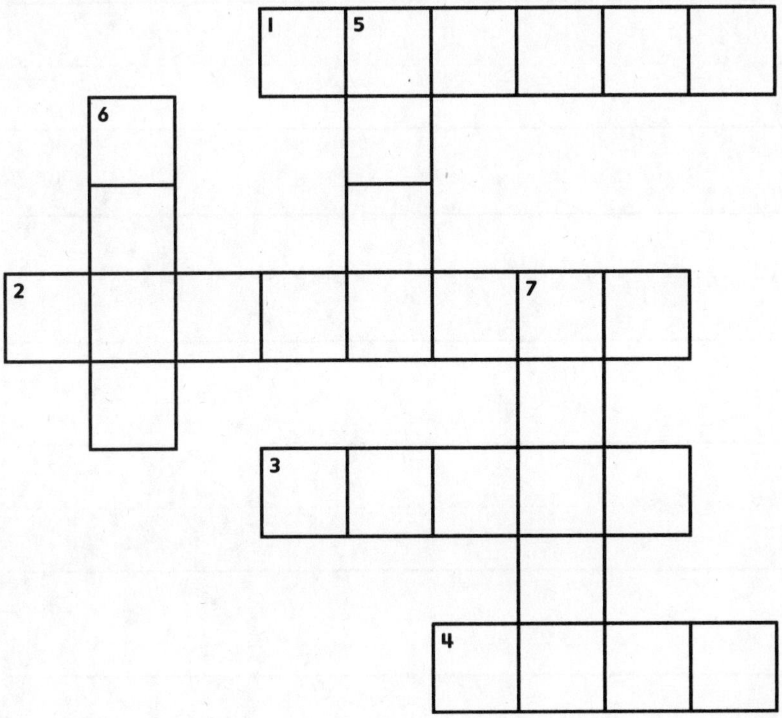

Across

1. you do this with water
2. what you like best
3. you do this with a partner
4. when you put something on

Down

5. two of the same thing
6. a big brown animal
7. 1 + 2

Name ______________________

Write a letter to your friend to thank them for something. Make sure you leave space between words and use commas correctly. Write neatly.

____

Date: ______________________

____

Dear ______________________

____

Thank you for ______________________

____

____

____

____

Your friend,

____

____

Name ______________________________

Some words have more than one syllable.

When a word has a vowel followed by r,
the vowel and r stay in the same syllable.

turtle = tur / tle   circus = cir / cus

target = tar / get   story = stor / y

Read the words. Make a check mark √ next to the word that has a vowel followed by r. Draw a line between the syllables in that word.

1. ______ turkey   ______ rocky

2. ______ rabbit   ______ market

3. ______ perfect   ______ pencil

4. ______ frozen   ______ forty

Name ____________________

A. Circle the word in each sentence that has a vowel followed by r. Write the syllables of the word below the sentence.

1. My sister and I are barely sleepy.

2. Mom will read us a story in bed.

3. It is a perfect way to end the day.

B. Use one of the words you circled above to write a new sentence.

Name ______________________________

Read the words in the box out loud. Complete each sentence. Use one of the words in the box.

favorite	few	gone	surprise	wonder	young

1. We will ____________ Mom when she comes home.

2. Spot is a very ____________ puppy.

3. I like grapes, but pears are my ____________ food.

4. There are only a ____________ books on my shelf.

5. I ____________ what time Dad's plane will land.

6. Mom made cupcakes, but they are all ____________ .

Name ______________________________

nation: A nation is a group of people living in one country.

unite: To unite is to join together.

A. Write unite or nation to finish each sentence.

1. This is the flag for our ______________________.

2. Our class will ______________________ with Mr. Tate's class to see the play.

B. Write a sentence using a word from the box.

difficult	nobody

____

____

Name ______________________________

Writers can use **metaphors** to help readers picture details. A metaphor compares one thing to another.

Example: The snow is a big white blanket.

Unlike a simile, a metaphor does not use <u>like</u> or <u>as</u>.

A. Read each sentence. Look at the underlined words. Then circle the sentence that tells how the two things are alike.

1. The <u>rainbow</u> is a <u>box of crayons</u> spilled from the clouds.

   Both have lots of colors.   Both are in a box.

2. The <u>cloud</u> is <u>cotton candy</u> floating by.

   Both are in the sky.   Both are fluffy.

3. The <u>oven</u> is a <u>dragon that breathes fire</u>.

   Both have heat inside   Both are very soft.

B. Circle the word that best completes the sentence. Write the word on the line.

4. Thunder is a ______________.

   bell   whistle   drum

Name ______________________________

An **adverb** is a word that tells more about a verb in a sentence.

Remember that a verb tells about action.

Some adverbs tell **how** an action happened. Many adverbs end in **-ly**.

Fran spoke <u>slowly</u>.

Circle the adverb in each sentence. Write it on the line.

1. The cat ran quickly up the tree. ______________

2. The band played loudly. ______________

3. Gram smiled sweetly when I gave the card I made. ______________

4. The wind blew strongly all night. ______________

Name ______________________________

A. Read the draft model. Circle the spelling the errors.

Draft Model

A snail crawled in the grass.

A haare hopped by the flowers.

"Spring is my favrite time of the year!" I said.

B. Now revise the draft by adding adverbs to each sentence. Fix the spelling errors you circled.

____

____

____

____

____

____

Connect to Writing

C. Look in your writer's notebook. Make sure you use adverbs correctly.

Name ______________________________

Use **capital letters** and **periods** in name titles.

Example: **Mr**. Drake **Mrs**. Chan
Ms. Baker **Dr**. Clark

Write each sentence correctly.

1. I will see dr Finn next May.

____

2. Mr and mrs Kent came to our house for lunch.

____

3. Next week, ms. Lu will be our new coach.

____

4. Do you know mrs. Park from the book store?

____

Birthdays are favorite days to share, too. Many young children have parties and wear a hat. What is your favorite day?

Connect to Community: Have children talk to a family member about their favorite day of the year.

(4)

Favorite Days

Do you have a favorite day of the year? There are many special days. We celebrate each in special ways.

Teacher Directions: Have children establish a purpose for reading the take-home story.

(1)

New Year's Day is the first day of the year. Some families stay home and play games together. They wonder what the new year will be like.

Mother's Day is in May. Father's Day is in June. Children take care to do something special for their moms and dads.

My Strategies and Tools

Student-Centered Learning

As children begin to learn the skills and strategies that help them think critically as they read, write, and participate in discussions and group projects, it is important to give them independent opportunities to apply what they learn.

How to Use the Blackline Masters:

1. Provide a blackline master to children and review as you explicitly teach the corresponding lesson.

Listen Carefully	Start Smart Week 1, S12
Ask Questions	Start Smart, Week 1, S16
Relevant Details	Start Smart Week 1, S80
Respond to a Text	Start Smart Week 1, S16
Retell a Text	Start Smart Week 1, S23
Parts of a Book	Start Smart Week 1, S30
Create a Picture in Your Mind	Start Smart Week 3, S80
Choose a Book	Start Smart Week 3, S97
Make a Connection	Unit 1 Week 1, T15
Research Plan	Unit 1, Week 1, T56
Combine Information	Unit 1 Week 2, T117, T119, T123
Who Is Telling the Story?	Unit 1 Week 2, T128
Make Inferences	Unit 1 Week 3, T199, T201, T205
Make a Prediction	Unit 2 Week 1, T22
Check Your Prediction	Unit 2 Week 1, T22

2. After teaching the lesson, ask children to discuss the blackline master during small group independent time.
3. Display the blackline masters in the reading center. As you assign independent work, direct children's attention to a specific blackline master to review.

Listen Carefully

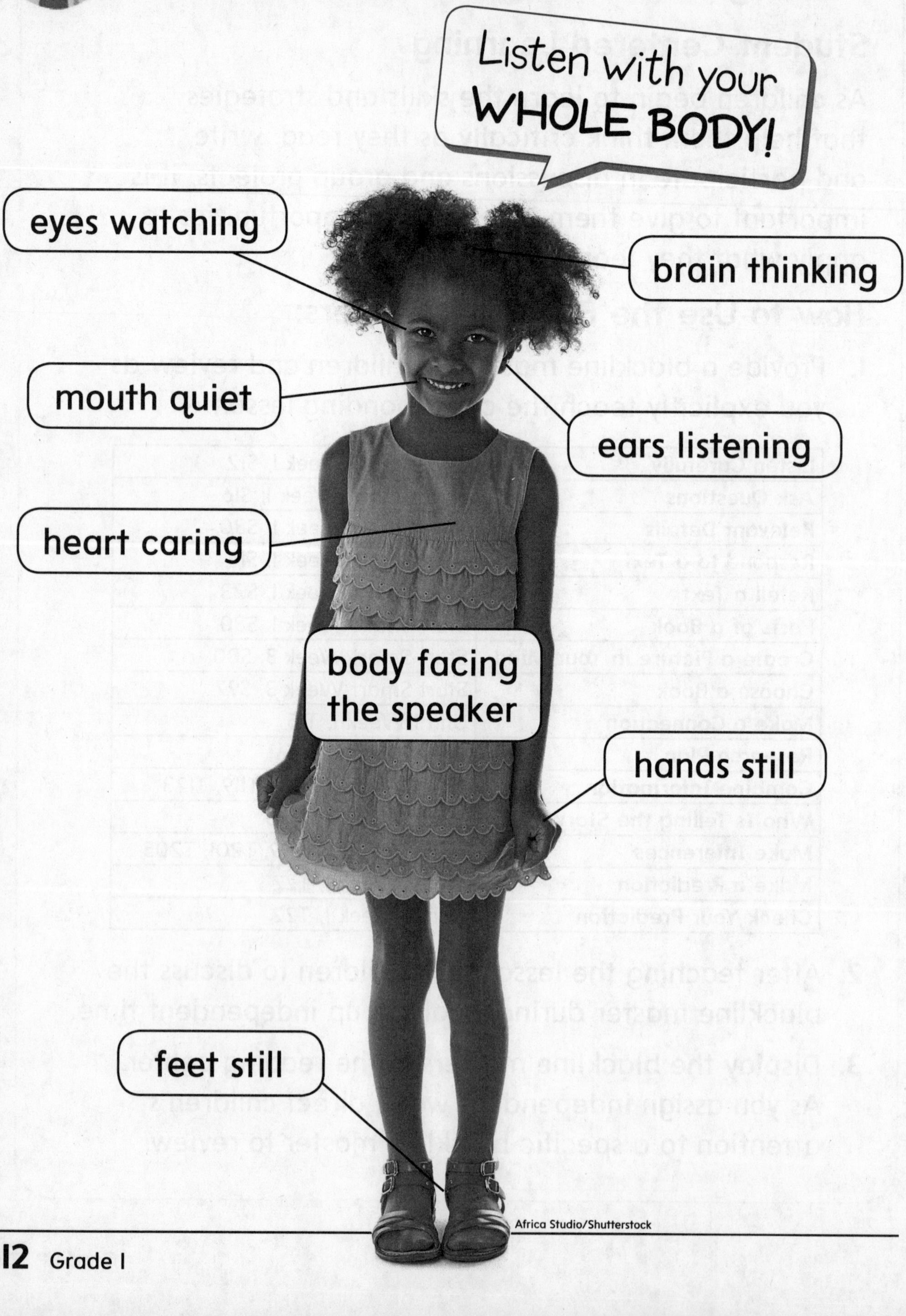

Africa Studio/Shutterstock

Ask Questions

Asking questions can help you understand what you read.

Before

Ask about

- the title, art or photos.
- what you will find out.
- what you want to understand.

During

Ask about

- ideas you do not understand.
- words you do not know.
- the characters in a story.
- an event from a text.

After

Ask about

- something you still want to understand.
- more information you want to know.

Relevant Details

Relevant details are the most important details. Find relevant details in the text, pictures or photos.

Spot is Jim's best friend.
Jim and Spot like to run.
Jim and Spot like to jump.
They have fun together.

Relevant Details

Spot is Jim's best friend.
They have fun together.

Read a text with a partner.
Talk about the details.
Identify the relevant details.

Respond to a Text

Share what you learn about a text. Use text evidence in your response. Make a connection to the text. Use new words you learned.

Talk About It

- Talk to a partner.
- Discuss the topic. Talk about what the text is about.
- Tell how you connected to the text.

Write About It

- Write complete sentences.
- Read your writing.

Draw a Picture

- Write labels.
- Talk about your picture.

Retell a Text

Retelling a text can help you understand the story. Take turns with a partner retelling a story.

Fiction	Nonfiction
Remember to think about what happens at the beginning, middle, and end when retelling a fiction text.	Remember to use the topic and relevant details to retell a nonfiction text.

Parts of a Book

Front Cover

Title: the name of the book

Author: the person who wrote the book

Illustrator: the person who drew the pictures

Table of Contents

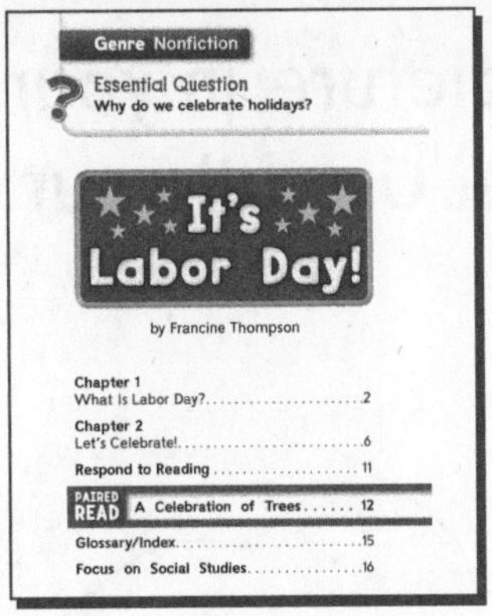
Genre Nonfiction

Essential Question
Why do we celebrate holidays?

It's Labor Day!

by Francine Thompson

The table of contents tells the page numbers for each part of the book.

Glossary

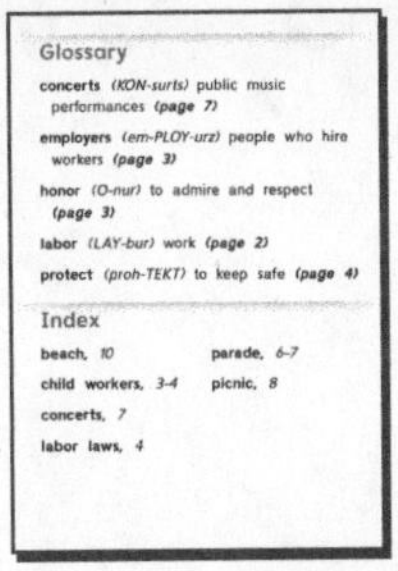
Glossary

concerts *(KON-surts)* public music performances ***(page 7)***

employers *(em-PLOY-urz)* people who hire workers ***(page 3)***

honor *(O-nur)* to admire and respect ***(page 3)***

labor *(LAY-bur)* work ***(page 2)***

protect *(proh-TEKT)* to keep safe ***(page 4)***

Index

The glossary gives the definition of words in the book. It tells how to pronounce the words, too.

Back Cover

The back cover can tell information about the book. It can have illustrations or photos.

Create a Picture in Your Mind

Think about the text as you read.

Create a picture in your mind as you read each page. Use all your senses.

I see ...

I hear ...

I can smell ...

I can taste ...

I can touch ...

Choose a Book

How to choose a book:

- Pick a book. Open it to any page.
- Read all the words on the page.
- Put one finger up for each word you can't figure out.

Five Finger Rule

	0 – 1 Fingers	This book will be easy for you. Make sure you don't choose too many books that are too easy for you.
	2 – 3 Fingers	This is a great choice!
	4 Fingers	Give this book a try.
	5 Fingers	This is a challenging book. You might want to make another choice.

Now spend time reading. Try to read a little longer each time.

Make a Connection

Make a connection to what you read.
Share your connection with a partner.

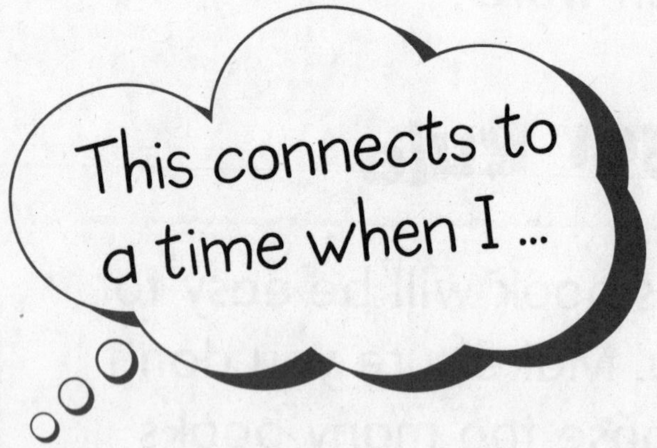

Research Plan

Follow the steps.

Step 1

Choose a topic.

- What do you want to find out about?

Step 2

Write your questions.

- What do you want to learn?

Step 3

Decide where to find the answers.

- Talk to an expert or read a text.
- Find the information you need.

Step 4

Write what you learn.

- Draw pictures.
- Write the answers to your questions.

Step 5

Choose how to present your work.

Create a model.

Write about your topic.

Do a demonstration.

Share what you learned!

Combine Information

Each page of a text gives you information. The information on every page is connected. Sometimes new information can change what you understand about a text.

"Yes, I do," said Crocodile.

"Then will you carry me on your back to the mainland?" asked Rabbit.

"No!" said Crocodile. "If you leave this island we cannot play together. You must stay here."

8

+

Chapter 3

The Trick

After a while, Rabbit asked another question. "Crocodile, are there more rabbits or crocodiles in the world?"

"There are many more crocodiles than rabbits!" replied Crocodile.

"Do you think there are enough crocodiles to stretch from here to the mainland?" Rabbit asked.

9

+

"Of course!" shouted Crocodile. He told Rabbit that he would call his friends together and prove it.

Crocodile slipped into the water. In minutes, hundreds of crocodiles joined him.

They lined up tail to snout. They soon formed a bridge that stretched from the island to the mainland.

10

= What I Learned

- Read a page.
  Tell a partner what you learned.
- Read another page.
  Tell a partner what you learned.
  Did your understanding of the text change?
- Tell how the information is connected.
  Take turns with your partner.

Who Is Telling the Story?

Read or listen to the story. Talk about who is telling the story. Is the narrator a character inside the story or a speaker outside the story?

Narrator is a character in the story

Look for the words **I, me,** and **my.**

I saw **my** mom.

Narrator is a speaker outside of the story

Look for the words such as **he, she, they,** and **characters' names.**

Tom and Jan went outside. **They** saw a bird.

Make Inferences

Sometimes an author does not tell you some information.

- Think about clues in the text or pictures.
- Think about what you already know.
- Put the clues and what you know together.
- Make an inference.

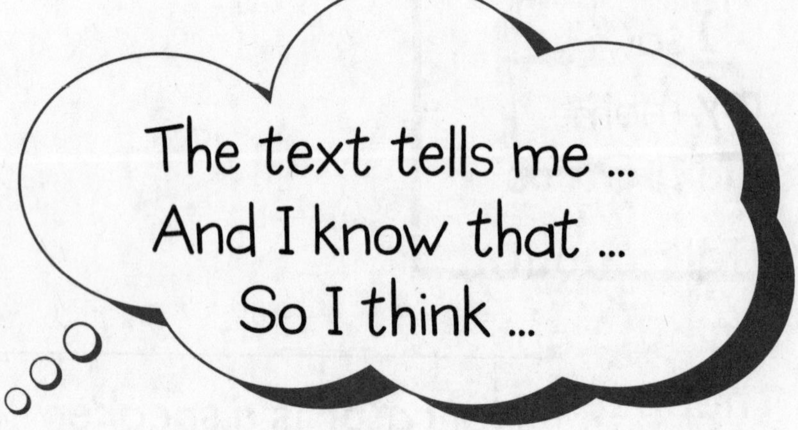

Make a Prediction

A prediction is a guess about what will happen next. To make a prediction you can use information from the text.

Text Features

Look at the photos and illustrations.

Look at the captions.

What information will you learn?

Text Structure

Talk about how the text is organized.

What happened first? What may happen next?

Genre

What is the type of text you are reading?

What will the characters do?

What may happen next?

Check Your Prediction

Check to see if your predictions are correct. If they are not correct, you can always change them.

Text Features

Look at the photos and illustrations.

Look at the captions.

What information did you learn?

Text Structure

Think about how the text is organized.

What happened?

Genre

What is the type of text you are reading?

What did the characters do?

What happened?